Time to Spare in
Victorian England

Time to Spare in Victorian England

JOHN LOWERSON

AND

JOHN MYERSCOUGH

 THE HARVESTER PRESS

THE HARVESTER PRESS LIMITED
Publisher: John Spiers
2 Stanford Terrace, Hassocks, Sussex

Time to Spare in Victorian England first published in 1977
by the Harvester Press Limited.

British Library Cataloguing in Publication Data
Lowerson, John
   Time to spare in Victorian England.
   Bibl. – Index.
   ISBN 0–901759–56–2
   1. Title   2. Myerscough, John
   301.5'7'094225   GV76.E6S/
✓ Recreation – England – Sussex – History

Photoset, printed and bound
in Great Britain by
REDWOOD BURN LIMITED
Trowbridge & Esher

Contents

List of Illustrations

between pages 88–89

PREFACE

This book began as a short series of talks and conversations for BBC Radio Brighton, given under the auspices of the University of Sussex's Centre for Continuing Education. John Spiers of the Harvester Press suggested that we make them the basis of an illustrated book.

In recent years, there has been a growth of interest among academic historians in the history of leisure and recreation. Whilst this book incorporates some of the results of that research, it is not an academic monograph, designed only for a specialist audience. Rather, it introduces the theme to general readers, who might include the sixth-former, first year undergraduates and students in adult education. Although it concentrates on the experience of change in Sussex, other parts of England have been introduced where a comparison is relevant, and it should, therefore, interest a wider audience. We must emphasize that, like the original radio programmes, it reports only aspects of the story and a few of the possible interpretations. Anything other than a simple introduction would have been premature at this stage in the development of the subject. Our hope is that our work will stimulate others to fill the gaps.

We could not have written it without a great deal of advice and practical help from many people. Our warmest thanks must go to Robert Thorne, but we also wish to mention with gratitude James Parr of the BBC,

Joan Astell of the Seaford Museum of Local History, Miss Baird and Miss Hollindale of the Brighton Reference Library and their staffs, Miss Robertson of Battle and District Historical Society, Judith Brent of East Sussex Record Office, Edward Reeves, Anthony Jenner, Martin Williams, Marcus Cunliffe, Robin Reeve, Penny Summerfield, John Hutchinson, Kevin Moloney, Rosemary Harris, Pat Bennett, Yvonne Wood and her staff, and MaryAnne Stevens, all of whom fetched, carried and dug out material for us and listened patiently to our sometimes bizarre requests. What we have done with their knowledge and assistance remains our responsibility.

JOHN LOWERSON
JOHN MYERSCOUGH
Brighton, 1977

ACKNOWLEDGEMENTS

We are grateful to the following for permission to use illustrations:
Battle and District Historical Society: 9, 23
Brighton and Hove Albion Football Club: 26
The British Library: 15
  East Sussex County Library –
  Brighton Reference Division: 1, 8, 11, 14, 16, 18, 24
  Hastings Reference Division: 6
  Hove Reference Division: 2, 12, 22
East Sussex Record Office: 10
Harvey and Son Lewes Ltd.: 5, 13
Robin Reeve: 3
Rothman's Ltd., The Frith Collection: 7
St John's College, Hurstpierpoint: 17, 25
The Sunday Times/Sussex Archaeological Society Reeves Collection: 4, 12, 19, 20

INTRODUCTION

Most of today's leisure habits and expectations remain staunchly Victorian. The nineteenth-century distinction between work and leisure, for example, still provides the basic polarities in our daily lives, and there is scarcely a single modern recreation that is not based on a prototype which dates from before the First World War. A history of leisure may, therefore, help us both to see our own society more clearly and also to become aware of the roots of our own recreational practices and beliefs about leisure.

In describing the changing perceptions and practice of leisure during the nineteenth century, we have been forced to take the view that there was in Victorian England a virtual 'leisure revolution'. This involved, amongst other things, three important social developments, a growth in the quantity of free time available, a growing array of new ways to fill the increasing hours of leisure time and associated changes in habits of spending on recreational activities. This book attempts to illustrate these developments with seven essays on selected aspects of leisure activity – seaside holidays, life at home, drinking, self-improvement, theatrical entertainment, music and games – preceded by a chapter dealing with some of the more general issues.

There was also a change in attitudes and this is why a book about leisure may seem to refer too much to work. In terms of the dominant Victorian work ethic spare

1

time became something to be earned by hard work, remission for good conduct, a reward for responsibility, and, for most people, the hours of work determined the hours of leisure. The word 'leisure' itself derived one of its possible meanings as 'time at one's own disposal' from the contrast with work. But the distinction between work and leisure, as it evolved in Victorian England, was neither absolute nor was it the same for each individual. Some saw the two activities as complementary aspects of the full life; others thought work a scourge, necessary or not; the rest, perhaps the majority, reversed these values and made leisure the demoraliser and work the true expression of the satisfying life. Apart from attitudes to leisure, there was the further problem of the nature of leisure activity itself, which depended less on the intrinsic character of a particular recreation than on the purpose and willingness with which it was undertaken, and this could vary. Thus, a game of football was work to the late Victorian professional player and a leisure activity to the amateur. Similarly, education was regarded as a suitably improving use of leisure time when undertaken voluntarily, in a mid-Victorian Mechanics' Institute, for example, and it ceased to be so regarded after the introduction of compulsory schooling later in the century. The loss of freedom of choice in the deployment of time made the difference.

Despite the many difficulties of definition in this context, two important Victorian achievements remain clear, and both of them were facets of the broader adjustment taking place between the slower rural past and the quickening life of the new industrial century. The first was the acceptance of a more or less clear-cut distinction in every-day life between work and leisure, quite different in its meaning and significance from the distinction between exertion and repose, which had prevailed in earlier days. The second achievement was the rationalisation of free time into a weekly and annual timetable of regular holidays and time off work, which again contrasted with the intermittent holy days of a previous period.

Leisure, further, became the subject of a crucial debate about how people should make use of their time, both for the good of their souls and for the good of their country. Reform and respectability came into all aspects of spare time for the Victorians, either to condemn or to encourage, and the old ways of pre-industrial England seemed coarse, brutal and predominantly vulgar. Their persistence threatened the very survival of Victorian progress – at least in the eyes of its most fervent disciples – and improving leisure could be used to transform the 'swinish multitude' into the 'respectable working classes'.

Apart from the issues raised in Chapter 1, several general themes occur throughout the book and so, perhaps, it would be useful to list them here. The improving use of leisure time, for example, is discussed directly in Chapter 7, but it is also an important feature, as one might expect, of the history of temperance and of athletics. The changing composition of the leisure class is sketched briefly in Chapter 1, but some of its effects, on the design of houses for example, are left for discussion later. A further factor in the evolution of leisure was social imitation, the subtle influence of which, not always for the better, can be traced in the history of games, choral societies and drinking. Some would argue that it also entered the music halls, but as an influence in the reverse direction, when those in high places learnt to enjoy entertainments of a socially inferior origin. Growing affluence meant a more varied array of commercial entertainments, from the rise of professional games to the proliferating theatres and flourishing holiday trades, elsewhere, if not in Brighton. Even the long-established drink trade was forced to change its commercial methods and objectives as a result of competition from new rivals as well as public criticism towards the end of the century. Finally, there is a general point about chronology. It can be argued that the most significant years of change, from the modern point of view, in the evolution of leisure provision were in the 1880s. Before this decade, the influence of commercial interests in the growth of organised leisure were counterbalanced by the activities of voluntary agencies, either to edify or to amuse. But now the government extended its responsibility into general education and the middle classes, their energies declining with their anxieties, withdrew somewhat from their altruistic involvement in improving organisations. At the same time, rising real wages meant that the initiative could swing to those seeking financial profit from leisure. And so the decade of the 1880s saw the voluntary bodies in moral decline, the fledgling State and flourishing private industry establish among themselves a new and somewhat uneasy power relationship, which still sets the basic context of leisure today.

This history of nineteenth-century leisure is set mainly in the county of Sussex. Since the authors live in the county, it was practical to make it the subject of a local case study, based on readily available sources,

4

which could both illustrate a method and provide a point for subsequent comparisons. The concentration on a single county also made good historical sense, because only by setting a geographical limit did it become possible even to piece together a moderately full account of the growing variety of uses of and attitudes to leisure time. Was the pattern of leisure in Victorian Sussex distinctive to the county? Its large and remote rural hinterland certainly gave the county a special flavour and the proximity to London, with its unique size and particular economic and social character, produce more than one contrast with other parts of the country. The coastal resorts of Sussex, for example, unlike the resorts of the North, rarely attracted working men to stay away from home on holiday. Other special local features spring to mind – the apprentice activity which persisted in the bonfire rituals of Lewes, the relatively late arrival in the county of professional football, the proliferation of weekend homes in the Weald – although the dearth of published studies of other regions means that there can be little certainty in most of these comparative matters. In some respects, indeed, the variety of experience within the county cancels out the interest in external comparisons. Brighton, as the largest town in Sussex, was far from typical of the county as a whole and there is an important distinction to be drawn between this town and the less garish, new resorts along the coast. Different again were the settlements inland, where recreations remained under the influence of surviving local traditions and the more limited scope for commercial developments.

It is easier to see the nineteenth century in Sussex through the eyes of reformers than it is to provide direct evidence of popular reactions to the new life styles that were being developed. There were no mass observation agents, television reports or opinion polls to ask how the man in the Battle back street felt about things and even the new tools of oral history could be used only to illuminate the final phases of our story. Such records as do survive are often the ephemera, the posters and postcards, that show us comparatively little, only the surface of what took place. Many aspects of leisure are, therefore, not covered in this book and, indeed, much more research and a much bigger book would be necessary fully to explain the massive redirection of individual and societal energies which the Victorian development of leisure entailed. Some of these developments were more successful than others, both morally and commercially, and we try to explain the reasons for the differences. The faces and poses of some of the characters in the photographs reproduced in this book may look stilted and arrogant. But the Victorians were rightly proud of realising, at least in part, their dream of leisure which we today, for all our apparent prosperity, dash and sophistication, have only succeeded in modifying and extending.

CHAPTER 1

TIME TO SPARE

Work was the dominant Victorian social ideal, and worthy, meaningful toil was one of the critical standpoints from which leisure came to be viewed. Samuel Smiles, for example, that stern apostle of work, warned,

> An easy and luxurious existence does not train men to effort or encounter with difficulty, nor does it awaken that consciousness of power which is so necessary to energetic and effective action in life.[1]

Yet in the late Victorian and Edwardian period those people in the happy position of not needing to work were more numerous, at least relatively, than at any time before or since. Even the very large numbers of modern pensioners have rarely stopped work from choice. In 1891, for example, the equivalent of 4 per cent of the occupied population were heads of households living on private means. For Sussex the comparable figure was 7.6 per cent and this concentration of a 'leisure class' in the county enabled the development of leisure industries catering for the changing tastes of this class, whether for the spa life of the eighteenth century or for the plutocratic displays and contrasting private domestic comforts of the nineteenth century.

A life of leisure was not necessarily idle. Whilst all members of the leisure class were free from the need to work, by no means all of them avoided arduous responsibilities. For example, the eighteenth-century gentleman, never thinking of himself as 'employed', frequently 'worked' hard in politics, the law and farming. In contrast, the late Victorian leisure class, with its money often inherited from industrial and commercial forbears, undertook fewer public responsibilities. Some of the latter, embarrassed by the 'Gospel of Work', cowered in comfortable suburban privacy or swanned on distant shores away from public disapproval; others, after an earlier life of Samuel Smiles' energetic and effective action, flaunted their wealth and ease to demonstrate the rewards that good behaviour could bring. All these groups remained a minority. Below this permanently leisured stratum of society, however, changes took place which transformed the context and character of leisure pursuits for those who had to work and gave almost everybody some leisure or regular time to spare.

In earlier centuries the rhythm of life in the rural world was determined mainly by the cycle of the farming year. Weather and seasons set appropriate work loads which varied the intensity of labour from week to week. The turning points of the agrarian year were marked by large and small festivals and saints' and holy days punctuated the progress of every month. This rhythm also shaped the life of the towns, and even the Bank of England was closed for 47 weekdays in 1761. Essential rural economic activities such as fairs were often intertwined with leisure occasions. Recreation and play fitted into this overall pattern of intermittent work and found their roots in existing community relationships. Hunting, horse racing, pugilism, cockfighting and cricket, all depended on support from the

8

gentry, whilst the publicans, running the principal communal institutions in the village, brought in itinerant entertainers, organised the betting and provided the space for indoor games. Drinking, indeed, was an intrinsic feature of most recreational activities. Some of these occasions, like the wakes, were opportunities for extravagant excess and licentious fun; others saw traditional social rules inverted for the day. The variety of physical recreations was wide, from very loosely organised team games, such as the many versions of football – some, but not all, dangerous – to multifarious bloodsports, which asserted the essential authority of man over hostile and raw nature, albeit represented as it usually was by some mangy, tethered animal. There was, however, another, more 'progressive' side to the eighteenth century. The above picture understates the influence of civilised and orderly towns, the considerable migration to and from rural England and the beliefs of 'the industrious sort of people' in the value of systematic, hard work. The latter was to grow, especially among those gentry who were hostile to idle customs. But for the 90 per cent of the Sussex population still living in the countryside in 1801, the ancient intermingling of work and play and of recreation and drink were still the norm, and the tidy contrasts of a later age between work time and leisure time were as yet unknown.

An important change in the pattern of recreations occurred during the period of the industrial revolution itself. This was the eradication of most of the riotous and cruel bloodsports and recreations of the countryside, together with the elimination of most of the wakes and traditional holy days from the calendar, a process virtually completed by the 1840s. Indeed, the Bank of England's 47 weekday closures had fallen to 4 by 1834. This development is commonly attributed to the specific demands of the new manufacturing civilisation, and it is easy to see how customary holidays were thought to waste valuable working time and leave expensive industrial plants unused. Irregular timekeeping, drunkenness and dissipation were rightly felt by many employers to be inconsistent with effective work. Indeed, alongside powerful voluntary associations such as the Society for the Prevention of Cruelty to Animals (founded 1824) and the Lord's Day Observance Society (founded 1833), industrialists were prominent in the fight against traditional life styles. Bloodsports attracted the most passionate attention, and between 1800 and 1838 eleven Bills against cruelty to animals were presented in Parliament. But effective reform depended very much on local conditions and particularly on the possibility of organising 'respectable' opinion at all levels of local society. In Sussex, for example, cock scailing died out after the 1780s yet ancient football still survived a century later.

The campaign against sports reached even the non-industrial counties and the widespread disappearance of traditional recreations supports the view that there were other causes for this transformation, in addition to the growth of manufacturing activity, confined as this was to a few parts of the country. It must be remembered, however, that even the non-industrial counties were influenced by the economic and social consequences of the industrial revolution. While Sussex, for example, was far removed from the immediate scene of the industrial revolution with its popular symbols, the

10

new industries in coal, iron and cotton centred on the Midlands and the North, the county felt the strong impact of rising incomes, the increasing importance of towns and the growth of new occupations, each the indirect result of industrialisation. New industrial attitudes also appeared everywhere in the wake of the new manufactured products. Thus, by 1911, Sussex had become a relatively prosperous county with 70 per cent of its residents living in towns, and its workers in agriculture reduced to 12 per cent of the labour force. Indeed, between 1821 and 1831, Brighton had been the fastest growing town of over 20,000 inhabitants in Britain, an achievement more than comparable with the industrial giants of the north.

These changes had obvious implications for recreations. The very size of the enlarged towns, manufacturing centres or not, meant that older leisure styles had to change. Riotous behaviour was a much greater threat to public order and private rights in crowded streets of towns than in the fields and commons of countryside. Sydney Smith, the Dean of St. Paul's, commented ironically on another social aspect of the campaign against sports.

> The real thing which calls forth the sympathies and harrows up the soul, is to see a number of boisterous artisans baiting a bull, or a bear; not a savage hare or a carnivorous stag, but a poor, innocent, timid bear, not pursued by magistrates, and deputy lieutenants, and men of education, but by those who must necessarily seek this relaxation in noise and tumultous merriment, by men whose feelings are blunted, and whose understanding is wholly devoid of refinement.[2]

A general softening of manners in England between

11

1780 and 1850 also helps account for these altered attitudes to violent sports. In Professor Perkin's words, there was a 'moral revolution' during which Britain 'ceased to be one of the most aggressive, brutal, rowdy, riotous, cruel and blood-thirsty nations in the world and became one of the most inhibited, polite, orderly, tenderminded, prudish and hypocritical'.[3] Thus, public order, crowded towns, refined sensibility and the evangelical conscience were as much the enemies of old habits as was industrial efficiency.

Employers, particularly industrialists, were successful during the nineteenth century in establishing new patterns and hours of work which entailed changes in the quantity and quality of leisure. Rural overpopulation and rising food prices forced many men to forsake the traditional life for the towns and industrial villages, which offered work with higher pay but longer hours and little time off. In Sussex this change was delayed more than elsewhere but Brighton and the other coastal towns still drew in the labourers from what had become by the middle of the century one of the poorest agricultural areas in England. After the new locomotive and carriage works was opened in Brighton in 1852, for example, there were jobs to be filled for eventually 3,000 men. The work was regular, the hours were long, but the pay made it worthwhile.

Continuous hard work put a premium on free time which came to be seen as the obverse of work, namely leisure. But the long hours of unremitting work were basically confined to a few of the industrialised trades and to a relatively short period of time. Even in this kind of employment, the stipulated hours of work were eventually reduced, especially in the second half of the nineteenth century. Reductions were generally achieved in Britain by voluntary agreements and State regulation only affected women and children, who were regarded as unfree agents in need of protection. The major exception in our period was the Coal Mines Act of 1908, which made obligatory the eight-hour day for miners. During the 1820s and 1830s a 72-hour week had operated in the best textile factories of the North, but the concentrated employment of women and children in this trade attracted Parliamentary attention and a 60-hour week was established by law after 1850, which was further reduced to 56 hours in 1874. Under the influence of this legislation, the hours for men were similarly reduced and a 54-hour week became common by the 1880s. By 1914 it could be said that 52 hours was the normal load for skilled workers in the organised trades. In the reduction of hours long periods of slow progress were followed by abrupt changes. The timing of changes was sometimes associated with slack trade, as in the late 1840s and the late 1900s, both periods when legislation about hours of work was enacted. Reductions were also associated with times of high employment, in the 1870s, for example, when the nine-hour day came in for building workers, and in 1919–20, when very widespread reductions took place.

This picture of falling hours of work has concerned nominal hours in the regular trades. It should be pointed out, however, that the actual hours of work were often less than this, as they were affected by fluctuations in the trade cycle, the weather and the seasons of the year. Absenteeism was also a problem since, even in the most modern factories, the older traditions were observed, such as St. Monday – the practice of taking

13

Monday off work to recover from the weekend's drinking – which persisted into the twentieth century. Annual holidays, some with pay, were also introduced, further to qualify the misleading picture of endless work.

With the adoption of an industrial mode of work, the fundamental valuation of time itself also changed. The practice of clocking-in at work and the affixing of clocks to public buildings after the 1840s provided ways to measure wasted time and the means to save it. It is hardly surprising that many towns, including Brighton and Hastings, chose to celebrate Victoria's Jubilee by the erection of new clock towers.

Several important categories of the Victorian work force, however, never surrendered totally to the new economy of time. Despite the industrial revolution, a great deal of manufacturing activity was performed, not in large factories, but in small-scale workshops and by outworkers, independent of the world of regulated hours and of organised labour. Outworkers could decide the time and duration of their work, as could the skilled craftsmen, who were generally in such scarce supply that they could readily stipulate the hours that they preferred to work. Agricultural labourers too found their work styles little changed. In Sussex mechanisation made little difference to local farming until the very end of the nineteenth century. In the 1830s as much as a quarter of the county's farm labourers was underemployed – 'leisured', but glad of work at most times of the agricultural year. By the 1890s, however, the new shortage of labourers meant that agricultural workers could begin more to stipulate their conditions of work.

14

The casual workers were another critically important, if diminishing, group whose attitudes came in for the full weight of Victorian criticism. They worked only when the opportunity occurred or when they chose to. Some rejected the work ethic in its entirety, preferring to work less and earn little. Alfred Marshall, the economist, explained this behaviour thus:

> It depends on the individual, whether with growing pay new wants arise . . . or he is soon satiated with those enjoyments that can be gained only by work, and then craves more rest . . . for activities that are themselves pleasurable . . . experience seems to show that the more ignorant and phlegmatic of races and of individuals, especially if they live in a southern clime, will stay at their work a shorter time, and will exert themselves less while at it, if the rate of pay rises so as to give them their accustomed enjoyments in return for less work than before.[4]

These 'ignorant' and 'phlegmatic' values were also recorded in the evidence to the Select Committee on Habitual Drunkards which was told in 1872 that,

> . . . drinking exists to this terrible excess because a workman can afford to lose one or two days a week, and yet make a great deal more money than ordinary labourers.[5]

It was a paradox of nineteenth-century economy that the relatively high cash rewards given for work in towns made survival easier for that section of the labour force which remained traditionally hostile to continuous hard work, albeit sweetened with regular time off.

The largest local group of workers outside the system of regulated hours consisted of the domestic servants, so essential to the semi-leisured life of the middle classes. Victims of the tyranny of the family and the rhythm of

15

domestic life, rather than the power of the machine and the logic of capital, their hours of leisure were terribly brief. George Moore's Esther Waters may have found life as a servant at Shoreham more than kind, but for servants in general, leisure was only experienced second-hand through the life style of those they served. Later in the century, the new white-collar workers, in their respectable eagerness to emulate their betters, seemed keen to accept the discipline of hard work for the financial rewards it brought. Indeed, it was probably the demands of the shop, good service and office discipline as much as machine-based manufacturing industry which eventually imprinted work indelibly on the mind of the Victorian labour force.

Thus, anxiety about the interaction between prosperity, drinking and attitudes to work provoked much Victorian moralising on the abuse of free time. Conscious of the growing quantity of time to spare and the social significance of its use, the mid-Victorian generations campaigned vigorously for 'rational' recreations, establishing numerous institutions of 'improvement'. The problem of the Victorian 'leisure revolution' was not the modern nightmare of an abyss of empty hours impossible to fill, but rather the difficulty of ensuring the proper exercise of moral responsibility in developing activities to occupy this free time. Previous anxieties about public order and 'idle custom' were reinforced by the continuing expansion of towns and the increasing use of the public house, the centre of idle recreation in the old world. The principal fear was that without the 'moral' improvement of the masses the conjunction of higher piece-rates and more spare time seemed perilously to threaten public order and industrial efficiency.

16

Competing agencies thus battled across the field of leisure for 'moral' control of life outside work as the choice between 'improving' recreation and its seductive alternatives became as important as the attitude to work itself in forming the industrial frame of mind.

Improving recreations took many forms. The dearth of regular exercise in smoky towns, for example, encouraged the pursuit of bodily fitness and healthy diet – enthusiasms which could have become obsessively puritanical, but which in general fostered the rise of temperance and innocent interests in athletic recreations, gymnastics and excursions to the invigorating seaside. Of course excursions could also occasion drunken indulgence, but Frederick Gale was in no doubt in 1885 of the benefits of physical exercise, which he thought,

> . . . has converted the employees, who from crowds and constant late hours in cities and large towns have degenerated into effeminate men . . . into fine, manly young fellows of pluck and sinew.[6]

Facilities for mental improvement were similarly developed, often with aristocratic or middle class assistance. Simple academic instruction, serious entertainment, lectures, discussions and debates were provided on a mutuality basis or by the new Working Men's Clubs, Institutes and a wide variety of Friendly Societies. Many industrial employers used mental improvement to serve the purposes of work; for example, Robert Owen in New Lanark and the Strutts of Belper in 1812 and the 1820s respectively laid on musical instruction for their employees.

Further influences affected the evolution of mid-

Victorian recreations. It fell to Britain as the first large, urbanised country in the world to develop recreations suitable for use in towns. The limits on space and time in the crowded conditions of Victorian towns required the adoption of games and entertainments, for participants and spectators alike, which were brief in duration and sparing in their use of land. Thus, the game of football travelled from the open spaces of the countryside via the restricted playing fields and congested timetables of the public school to the confines of the local town grounds. Also, the interplay of influences on recreation between the countryside and the town was another important factor. The very speed of British urbanisation strengthened the sense of a lost rural world. Nostalgia and the fondness of the rich for country living kept many rural themes alive in the imagery and practice of recreation. As migrants from the countryside to the town brought with them country interests which persisted in the towns, gardening and the raising of domestic animals among others, so townsmen moving to the country villages supported rural institutions, such as hunting and fairs, which might otherwise have faded away. From the 1860s onwards, there was also a more sophisticated reinterpretation of the countryside in its use for athletic recreations such as mountaineering, cycling and cross-country running.

Historians of Victorian leisure, however, must beware of drawing too sharp or facile a contrast between the 'traditional' and 'modern' worlds. The persistence into the industrial age of 'traditional' attitudes to work has already been described and, by the same token, new recreations were also capable of being slotted into the older timetable where this survived.

Thus, St. Monday was a popular day for railway excursions. There were also examples of traditional recreations persisting even into the twentieth century, especially those associated with country festivals, such as Whitsun or May Day. Moreover, although the bulk of bloodsports was eradicated, this did not produce sharp discontinuity with the past, a vacuum in the history of recreation, for new pastimes quickly took the place of the old and important recreational elements from the past, the pubs and horse racing, for example, not only survived but flourished in the industrial age, ensuring thereby a strong connection with the past. Thus, Victorian England was a varying mixture of continuity and change, a plural society in which existing community relationships continued to provide a powerful organisational basis for recreations. Both the physical environment and rhythm of life were undergoing sustained changes, but the social strength of new communities of work must be emphasised; few events in the 'traditional' world could have been more 'corporate' or 'organic' than a work's excursion to the seaside. Local community life was also nurtured by the pubs, improving institutes and manifold clubs of Victorian England and even the new types of commercial entertainment, such as professional football, exploited strong community feelings, rather than destroyed them, in the pursuit of profit.

The speedy growth of Victorian towns not only enlarged the available range of recreations but also set some limits to their enjoyment. Greater social differentiation in places of residence, for example, as well as the variety of places and times of work constrained the ways in which some individuals could spend their spare

time. Yet many Victorians also managed to pursue recreations across both space and class boundaries.
Many working men had been willing collaborators in
the campaign against disorderly recreations, but rough
sports and the race track continued to be followed by
high- and low-born alike, and, whilst income obviously
affected the size of stakes, it did not seem to affect the
enthusiasm for betting. Drink and temperance found
supporters in all classes. From their earliest days the
music halls attracted both the swell working-man and
the raffish aristocrat. In holiday-making, both respectable and rough resorts were ranged along the coast,
each catering for its own kind of visitor. The less dramatic examples of cultural harmony across the indeter-
minate boundaries between classes were also highly
significant, the mingling of like minded artisans and
shopkeepers in the Foresters and Buffalo Lodges, for
example. Social emulation was yet another strong
influence which countered the distinctions of class
and income in recreational activity and keep-
ing-up-with-the-Victorian-Joneses was given a great
boost in the late nineteenth century by the growth of the
white-collar occupations – teaching, clerking and nurs-
ing.

Thus, in the history of Victorian recreation the distinction must be drawn between two 'leisure cultures',
the 'respectable' and the 'rough', which can also be said
to have countermanded the divisions between classes.
Occasionally the separate elements in these two cultures became intertwined, much to the confusion of
contemporaries; witness the perplexed temperance
advocates faced with pubs which ran savings clubs and
meeting halls. Yet, in general, all the Victorians, those

who worked as well as those who did not, were required to make a basic cultural choice; whether to be drunk or sober, free-spending or thrifty, self-indulgent or self-denying, complacent or improving in their approach to life.

The significance of this moral distinction lessened towards the end of the century. The drink trade, for example, worked hard to make itself respectable and even the music hall ceased pandering to low taste and became 'an innocent and not undesirable form of amusement'. Much of the guilt was being taken out of fun. The ideological life of many voluntary associations also declined as the issues became less ardent and the causes less urgent. Few now regarded free time solely as a standing invitation to vice. After the 1880s many of the interested parties were prepared to leave improvement in the hands of the State educational system, which was already superseding some of the functions of the voluntary improvement institutions. Middle-class patrons of temperance clubs withdrew their active support at the same time as working men began taking control of their own clubs. Pressure of a different kind was also felt by the clubs as a consequence of the growing affluence in Victorian England, which encouraged enterprise and innovation in commercial entertainment and established rival attractions to the activities of clubs and societies. The growth in commercial entertainment can be seen from the employment it created; whilst the population rose on average by 0.8 per cent a year between 1871 and 1911, employment in the arts and entertainment increased by 4.7 per cent a year in the same period.

By 1907, the average expenditure on leisure goods and services had risen to 16.6 per cent of the total –

drink accounting for 9 per cent. Despite a crisis in the life of many voluntary organisations a new range of bodies for young people developed towards the turn of the century as a result of the growing anxiety about their physical condition and the needs of Imperial defence. The Scouts and the Boys' Brigade were the most successful of these.

But, in general, moral considerations surrendered to commercial ones, a trend about which Beveridge still despaired in 1948.

> The business motive . . . is seen in continual or repeated conflict with the Philanthropic Motive, and has too often been successful . . . the business of football pools, dog tracks, and cinemas . . . (exploits) in different ways for personal gain the increased leisure of the people. . . . In former days there was a great alternative to the pursuit of gain. . . .[7]

These processes effectively established our own leisure patterns. Since 1920 the hours of work and free time have scarcely changed, apart from an increase in the length of annual holidays. In many ways, indeed, the twentieth century places a lower value on leisure than the nineteenth, typically preferring increases in income to more time off.[8] Satisfaction from leisure is sought today not be lengthening the free time available but by spending more money during the same limited amount of time. By reinforcing the need for longer working hours, leisure expenditure has made work its own servant. For many people work itself has become a more meaningful activity. If we have fears about our ability to fill our leisure time, they may derive less from too much time to spare and more from too little of our Victorian ancestors' sense of improving moral purpose when using the leisure time at our disposal.

CHAPTER 2

SEASIDE HOLIDAYS

Seaside holidays in their modern form first became established as an important social institution during the 1840s. The nature and appeal of holidays at the seaside, however, were both strongly influenced by the previous successes of the eighteenth-century spas, the social context and purpose of which had been different from that of the Victorian resort. Whereas in the nineteenth century mass holiday-making was based on the short moments of rest and refreshment for those who habitually worked, the practice of making protracted visits to spas had arisen as an integral feature of a previous 'leisured' and high society.

The English gentry traditionally lived more or less permanently in the countryside where they combined serious farming with administrative and judicial responsibilities, an arrangement unique in eighteenth-century Europe. Increasingly, country life involved regular visits to the local county town and as a consequence local fashionable Seasons grew up in imitation of the established London Season, which enabled the leading members of county society to cultivate each others' company and thereby reinforce their established social position. Since the eighteenth century was also a time of pressure for upward social mobility, these fashionable Seasons were also the occasion for the parvenu to display his wealth, his talents and his eligible daughters in the hope of admission to the ranks of fashionable society.

As centres for this social activity the old county towns quickly expanded, together with the spas, newly-built for the purpose, as they acquired shops, theatres, assembly rooms and a wide variety of other useful facilities. The spas, of course, specialised in providing medical treatment which obtained cures with mineral water inland and with sea water on the coast. The richest gentlemen built second homes in these local towns so that they could better enjoy the carefully graded circles of visitors, the gossip of the dinner parties and the marriage marts of the assembly room balls. Thus, in eighteenth-century England commercialised leisure began to be provided in 'consumer towns', both old and new, which flourished on the expenditure of the affluent landed classes and their imitators. Spas were a subclass of these consumer towns, distinguished by their distinctive mix of medical and social facilities. Bath was the outstanding example of an inland spa which attracted national attention and the fishing village of Brighthelmstone became its maritime rival. In Sussex Brighton was followed by its lesser imitators, Hothampton (the precursor of Bognor), Littlehampton, Worthing, Hastings and St. Leonards.

Brighton, indeed, was already a well-established, local centre for the Sussex gentry before its rise to national fame. Its subsequent apotheosis was the result not only of its proximity to London, but also of a chance enthusiasm for the town on the part of the Prince of Wales, who was accompanied on his visits for the Summer Season by most of the 'out court'. When 'Prinney' became Regent and later King, he kept his affection for the town, and so Brighton was given a further social boost by the seasonal presence of the 'in court' and the government. During the Revolutionary and Napoleonic Wars, fashionable regiments of soldiers were posted in the town and these, in their turn, attracted aspiring mothers with eligible daughters and hoards of London prostitutes on similarly venal business. Many of the officers returned to live in the town on pensions after the peace of 1815. Thus, by effectively satisfying the social needs of the ruling and leisure class, Brighton doubled its population between 1811 and 1821, and became the fastest-growing town over 20,000 inhabitants in Britain during the following decade.

Eighteenth-century visitors to the coastal spas of Sussex were attracted less by an aesthetic interest in the sea and more by its medical properties. Accordingly, the first promenades and terraces of houses were built inland, away from the coast. The Steine at Brighton, for example, was laid out as the town's new promenade in a north-south direction and Hothampton was established almost a mile inland. By the time of Brighton's rapid expansion between 1811 and 1831, however, attitudes to nature had been changed by the popularisation of the picturesque aesthetic and the taste for romantic painting, and so the new squares and terraces were now built facing the sublime and dreadful sea, from Brunswick to Kemp Town. A visiting American thought the squares a necessary protection against the weather.

These three-sided squares are all large, with an enclosed park in the centre, and in such a windy place as Brighton, form very snug and sheltered promenades to the slender-legged invalid, and the sail-carrying dame. Kemp Town . . . is the finest bit of Brighton in point of architecture, and in one of its plainest

25

houses lives the Duke of Devonshire.[1]

Another American described the social preoccupations of fashionable visitors.

> The modes of getting rid of time, which seemed to be the great end and object of all, were various. Some lounged into reading-rooms; some sat down deliberately in shops, to make the most of the little business they were blessed with; some had themselves weighed, and were able to judge of their relative condition. Thus was the burden of the day got rid of. In the afternoon all repaired, by common consent, to walk, ride, or drive along the ramparts by the seaside. There were a great many ladies on horseback, riding beautifully, and with the confidence of assured skill; some were unattended by gentlemen, being followed by their servants; there were two whom I noticed in a phaeton, quite alone, driving a very spirited pair of horses, which one of them managed with consummate ease and skill; two grooms in livery, and admirably well mounted, followed them at a distance, leaving them quite unembarrassed, and without the fear of being overheard, to make their remarks upon those who were passing. There was every species of equipage represented here, from the pony phaeton to the lumbering fly, which seemed ever on the ascent. . . . It would have been difficult anywhere to see a more brilliant spectacle.[2]

Yet with the death of George IV, improving communications and the rise of respectability the bubble burst for this fashionable resort. The *Royal Pavilion*, indeed, was sold in 1850 by Queen Victoria who hated Brighton and all it stood for, whilst the office of Master of Ceremonies was abolished. During the foreign travel boom of the 1820s the racier members of the aristocracy had discovered the more raffish and cheaper pleasure resorts of the continent. An indication of the consequent decline in Brighton's appeal was the long delay in the completion of the building of the Kemp Town Estate during the 1830s and 1840s. Yet it was at this moment of transition in 1841 that Dr. Granville still found Brighton enchanting in a famous description of the place.

In the simplicity of my heart, I bethought me that as people are sent hither to enjoy the sea air for their health, they would be found at early morn pacing the grand parade; but early rising is not among the customs of the place. At seven o'clock I never observed a decent-looking person out of doors, and between that hour and nine, those only would be seen abroad who drove, walked or crept along to the German spa. . . . But when the glorious planet [the sun] lights up the two cliffs, and sheds its genial warmth on places of public resort, the terraces, the piers and walks – when the pedestrians and their fair mates – when the equestrian groups, and the 'fliers', and the numerous and handsome equipages come forth to parade along, and fill those haunts of fashion from the Junction Parade to Brunswick Square westwards, and again from the Albion Hotel to Kemp Town eastwards – oh, then Brighton is enchanting! and so it is indeed during the autumnal months, and for many days in winter also; for which reason it is that the place has acquired great renown at that season, among invalids and wealthy idlers, and will continue to retain it, as long as the British Clime remains unchanged.[3]

Although much diminished the fashionable Season lingered long. As the century progressed, the Season both slipped back to the autumn away from the new summer developments, and also passed to those lower in rank, including many who had made good from the Victorian commercial and industrial expansion. Nevertheless, Brighton remained popular both with particular social cliques, the diplomatic set in the 1840s, for example, and during European wars in the late 1840s and the early 1870s, when the fashionable Season would reconvene.

The range of great visitors had in general diminished noticeably by the 1860s, but Arnold Bennett's Edwin Clayhanger could still find dazzle and opulence in Edwardian Brighton.

> As for Brighton, it corresponded with no dream. It was vaster than any imagining of it. Edwin had only seen the pleasure cities of the poor and of the middling, such as Blackpool and Llandudno. He had not conceived what wealth would do when it organised itself for the purpose of distraction. . . . He suddenly saw Brighton in its autumnal pride, Brighton beginning one of its fine weekends, and he had to admit that the number of rich and idle people in the world surpassed his provincial notions. For miles westwards and miles eastwards, against a formidable background of high, yellow and brown architecture, persons the luxuriousness of any of whom would have drawn remarks in Bursley, walked or drove or rode in thronging multitude. Edwin could comprehend lolling by the sea in August, but in late October it seemed unnatural, fantastic. The air was full of the trot of glossy horses and the rattle of bits and the roll of swift wheels, and the fall of elegant soles on clean pavements; it was full of consciousness of being correct and successful. Many of the faces were monstrously ugly, most were dissatisfied and querulous; but they were triumphant.[4]

In so far as the high life persisted in late Victorian Brighton it had a seedy and degenerate aspect. The structure of the great houses survived but individual properties were being converted into flats from the 1890s onwards. Even the large, plutocratic hotels were in a sense a cheap substitute for private houses, necessitated by the expense of keeping servants. Hotels became especially popular for short or weekend visits and it was more convenient, and cheaper to use the servants provided by the hotel than to move an entire household for a short stay in private accommodation. Hotels had also changed their character. Previously they had simply provided private suites of serviced rooms, but the newer hotels based their appeal on a wider range of services and facilities, such as public restaurants and smoking rooms. These 'grand hotels' attracted their clients, especially the *nouveaux riches*, with stagey, public rooms where self-important strangers had a chance to meet and parade themselves in a setting decorated with the latest in interior design and domestic technology. Brighton's *Grand Hotel* which opened its doors in 1864, was designed by Whichcord and boasted both a lift and an external fire-escape. But when King Edward VII stayed in Brighton in 1908, 1909 and 1910, it was not at an hotel, although his visits did lead to a 'famous reunion of the forces of society'. The list of fashionable visitors for 17 September 1910 included five dukes, four duchesses, one marquis, twenty-three earls, thirty-three barons and all the principal members of the Cabinet. It is hardly surprising, therefore, that the rediscovery of the attractions of 'London-by-the-Sea' doubled the sale of first-class single train tickets for the journey between London and Brighton in 1910.

Thus, leisured society established both the physical fabric of resorts and the fashionable taste for the sea which were exploited in the Victorian popularisation of seaside holidays for the middle classes and the development of excursions for the masses. One pre-condition of these developments was the rise of the annual holiday which was a direct result of the newly-established rhythm of work. The half-day was given by law to textile operatives in 1850 and to shop girls in 1912 and was claimed by all the other regular trades during this period. The annual holiday, however, was another result of the pioneering activities in the industrial North where enlightened and calculating employers acknowledged the traditional wakes as official holidays, in expectation thereafter of regular attendance at work by a contented work-force. Although holidays with pay did not become customary for manual workers before the Holidays with Pay Act of 1938, the professional and white-collar workers, heavily concentrated in London, commonly enjoyed a fortnight's paid holiday from as early as the 1870s; the clerks of the Royal Exchange Assurance enjoyed three weeks' holiday with pay after 1881. This experience – the annual holiday, the shortened working week and the weekly half-day's holiday– was unique in nineteenth-century Europe and does much to explain Britain's dominant influence in the development of new forms of recreation. Both the week by the sea and the day-excursion were very important for Sussex, but it was the excursion which created the greater popular excitement. The arrival of excursionists in Brighton also raised the question of the conflict between rough and respectable recreations, which became an acute 'bread and butter' issue to the town.

In 1857 *The Train* carried a piece called 'Brighton Out of Season' (sic) which described the

> . . . miserable sight [on a summer Sunday of] poor London artisans and their families who had been beguiled by a promise of 'Eight hours at the seaside' to come down at 3/6 each, to Brighton to all places in the world.[5]

The first excursion train from London to Brighton –
the line had been opened in 1841 – ran at Easter, 1844.
Three engines pulled thirty eight coaches and took four
and a half hours to make the run, a time soon cut to less
than two hours. The development of the excursion,
indeed, owed less to the building of the railway itself
and more to the introduction of attractive excursion
fares. In 1844 when the ordinary second-class return
fare was 9s. 6d., the fare at the excursion rate was only
8s., and you could travel third-class for 5s. The price of
excursions fluctuated during the rest of the century –
1850, 3s. 6d.; 1861, 2s. 6d.; 1865, 3s. 6d.; 1872, 3s.; and
at the end of the century, 5s. 9d. Thus, in the 1870s it
was possible to take a family of four to Brighton and
back for nine shillings, a sum not difficult to save for
poor artisans and much easier for their betters. It is,
therefore, not surprising that in 1870 the 'artful traffic
manager of the S. Coast railway' advertised 'Nine hours
at the seaside to the Spitalfields operatives' and recom-
mended 'Saturday 'til Monday to overworked clerks'.
The heyday of the excursionist was in the 1860s, when
as many as 30,000 would arrive on Whit Monday,
whereas by the 1900s Brighton could only attract
300,000 trippers in a whole year.

Excursionists were always a controversial element in
the holiday trade of any seaside town, particularly one
with pretensions such as Brighton. Excursions were
'improving', but excursionists were always 'rowdy'.
The Lord's Select Committee on the Bill for Regulating
the Sale of Beer on the Lord's Day received complaints
in 1847–8 about the drunken condition in which day
excursionists returned to London from Brighton on

Sunday evenings. For one critic, in 1870, the trippers seemed 'in every way [like] Mr. Matthew Arnold's definition of philistinism – coarse, vulgar, stupid.'[6] They escaped the epithet 'drunken' this time, but such words reveal strong fears about the effect of excursion-traffic on the town. Apart from the misuse of the Sabbath, 'rowdy excursionists' might spoil the image of the town, offend residents and frighten away the more respectable resident holiday-makers. *Punch* carried verses on the subject:

> What does he come for?
> What does he want?
> Why does he wander thus
> Careworn and gaunt?
> Up street and down street with
> Dull vacant stare,
> Hither and thither, it
> Don't matter where!
>
> What does he mean by it?
> Why does he come
> Hundreds of miles to prowl
> Weary and glum,
> Blinking at Kosmos with
> Lack-lustre eye?
> He doesn't enjoy it, he
> Don't even try!
>
> Sunny or soaking, it's
> All one to him,
> Wandering painfully –
> Curious whim!
> Gazing at china-shops,
> Gaping at sea,
> Guzzling at beer-shops, or
> Gorging at tea.

Why don't he stay at home,
Save his train fare,
Soak at his native beer,
Sunday clothes wear?
No one would grudge it him,
No one would jeer.
Why does he come away?
Why is he here?[7]

The railway company was eventually persuaded in the late 1860s, after pressure from the respectable residents, to effect 'a discrete revision of the excursion traffic'. The price of the day return ticket was raised which together with the growth of attractive alternative destinations on the coast '[improved] greatly the class of people who patronised the town in the summer months'.

The trippers probably brought few economic benefits to the town and this was one reason for their unpopularity. In 1862 a critic argued that 'as they remain in the town only a few hours this custom is of little advantage to any but the publican'.[8] Another forgot to mention even the money spent on drink, such was his rage; '. . . it is to yield to false sentiment to sacrifice the interests of the town to the rabble who are here today and gone tomorrow and leave nothing behind them but the injured feelings of friends and patrons'.[9] Most excursionists, indeed, probably sought entertainments that were free of charge. The beach was the important attraction. There they could watch or join the 'batheable children and the happy parents, the sand pails and wooden spades, the nurse maids, the donkey, the goat chaise and all the et ceteras of ordinary watering place life.'[10]

33

Doubtless a few excursionists paid for admission to the Chain Pier, the first of Brighton's piers, designed by Samuel Brown and opened in 1823, which developed as one of the earliest pleasure piers in the country. Before it was demolished by storm in 1896, the visitor to the pier might have enjoyed a promenade, listened to a band concert (sacred music on Sunday), gone sea bathing from its head, shopped at a souvenir kiosk and even paid to be photographed by the celebrated Alfred Sharp. Plans to replace the Chain Pier had begun with the Brighton Marine Palace and Pier Act 1888, but it was many years before this new popular pier was completed in 1899. Meanwhile, the West Pier had opened in 1866 to sophisticated designs by the leading engineer of piers, Eugenius Birch. With an admission price of 6d., it became the promenade for visitors with social aspirations. Three thousand patrons could sit on its open-air deck, that is before the pavilions, concert hall and theatre were added two decades later.

There was plenty to entertain excursionists with technological interests in the Brighton of the 1880s and 1890s. Magnus Volk's eccentric, electrical masterpieces, his railway and his 'daddy longlegs', were joined after 1887 by the 'motor rail' to the top of Devil's Dyke. When Mr. Hubbard took over the Dyke in 1893, he added further attractions, including a steep-grade funicular, 880 feet long with cars carrying fourteen passengers at three miles per hour, for 2d. single. The cableway, 1,200 feet long, was even better value, at 6d. return for the more exciting journey. As an out-of-town pleasure park, on the American model, however, the Dyke was developed before its time and never really captured public imagination.

34

In contrast to the frugal tripper, the resident family holidaymaker was a more welcome visitor to the towns on the Sussex coast. The week's holiday at the seaside was the dream of 'the poor professional man and the struggling governmental clerks . . . getting away from the stuccoed residences of surburban gentility'[11] and any family with an income of £100 a year might afford a holiday in September, before 'everybody came' in November. By the 1860s such holidays had become an established feature of family life and they were making distinct and heavy demands on the seaside. Unlike the visitors to the fashionable Season, Victorian family holiday-makers were more interested in nature rather than in society. The resort was a place for strengthening family bonds, resting from the office and indulging in the quiet and economical pleasures of the amateur botanist, antiquarian and geologist. Many preferred to rent a house while staying in a resort, but there were also the comforts of the new accommodation industry, with its boarding- and lodging-houses. Brighton had 800 such establishments in the 1870s. The prices could be extortionate, and one sardonic account in 1862 described a

> . . . sitting room and bedroom, including all extras except boot-cleaning, kitchen fire, parlour fire, gas in the passage, washing of linen, use of cruet and option of playing upon a spinet of four and a half octaves for the small charge of 30s. per week.[12]

Arnold Bennett painted a seedy picture of a Brighton boarding house in 1910.

> It resembled nothing reputable in his experience. All was

35

incomprehensible. The room into which she led him was evidently the dining-room. Not spacious . . . it was nearly filled by one long bare table. Eight or ten monotonous chairs ranged round the grey walls. In the embrasure of the window was a wicker stand with a withered plant on its summit, and at the other end of the room a walnut sideboard in the most horrible taste. The mantelpiece was draped with dark knotted and rosetted cloth; within the fender stood a small paper screen. The walls were hung with ancient and fairly modern engravings . . . all distressing in their fatuous ugliness. The ceiling seemed black. The whole room fulfilled pretty accurately the scornful scrupulous housewife's notion of a lodging-house interior. It was suspect . . . Obviously the house was small . . . and the entire enterprise insignificant. This establishment was not in the Kings Road, nor on the Marine Parade, not at Hove; no doubt hundreds of such little places existed precariously in a vast town like Brighton. Widows of course were in straits.[13]

The Census records of the period confirm that the lodging-house keepers of late nineteenth-century Brighton were predominantly women, mainly over the age of fifty, and included many widows. Bennett's intuition that 'widows were in straits' is further corroborated by the fall in the level, if not the number, of private incomes between 1870 and 1900, whether drawn from land or from equities. Running a lodging-house was one of the few ways in which women faced with financial stress or personal difficulties, could earn an independent means of support, whilst maintaining a large house, servants and a modicum of status. The result may have had its shabby aspect but when in 1879 Black's Guide *Where Shall We Go?* advised against a holiday at Brighton, it had other considerations in mind.

If one wishes while leaving London for the seaside, to change as little as possible one's London habits . . . Or if prolonged absence from the metropolis be out of the question . . . Or, lastly, if one's nerves have been somewhat overstrung, and one's digestion in consequence become decidedly troublesome, with low spirits, and all sorts of attendant horrors, then, again, Brighton, with its bracing, healthy atmosphere, its stately magnificence, and its fulness and flush of cheerful life, is a very good place, indeed . . . But it is not the place for quiet people, or poor people (except in so much as it is more cheaply reached than any other watering-place), or for people who, long in populous cities pent, yearn for the sight of greener trees, and fairer flowers, and fresher associations of all kinds. Brighton is not for these.[14]

At the same time Eastbourne was developing as one of several quieter rivals to the Queen of Watering Places along the coast. *Where Shall We Go?* in 1879 also explained that,

. . . the baths, chief inns and lodging houses . . . form an extremely neat and clean assemblage, in rows and terraces with a fine esplanade; the whole looking out on a truly magnificent view of the ocean, including Beachy Head in the near vicinity. The Grand Parade . . . forms an agreeable and fashionable promenade. A new pier is in course of construction, similar, although on a smaller scale, to the west pier of Brighton. These objects, with the extreme quiet and absence of the ordinary gaieties of watering-places, are among the more obvious characteristics of Eastbourne.[15]

Eastbourne still preserved this peaceful atmosphere in 1905 when the Queen Newspaper's *Book of Travel* described the resort.

Eastbourne is one of the most bracing and healthy South Coast towns; one of the best built; more select than Brighton, and more picturesque than St. Leonard's. Its water is good; its drainage satisfactory as far as any such arrangements can be; its choice of houses is considerable, yet it is not overbuilt. The class of resident is distinctly good, and the recreative character of the place makes one independent of its varied social life.[16]

Faced with the natural advantages and the placid society of Eastbourne, Brighton's size and gaiety, however faded, were now as much a competitive drawback as its stony beach and its glaring sunlight. Further, despite the efforts of the Council on behalf of resident and visitor alike, the deficiencies in Brighton's botanical attractions remained a by-word.

Along the Sussex coast an array of towns developed, each offering its own brand of seaside attractions, vying with the others in its different mix of natural and man-made facilities. In sharp contrast to cosmopolitan Brighton was a very minor competitor – Seaford. Although an enthusiastic newspaper editor in the 1890s once described it as 'an embryonic Brighton', the little town along the coast never aimed that high. Indeed, both its residents and its developers deliberately avoided anything that would resemble the range of Brighton's leisure provision.

Today (1904) it is, in the words of a modern author, a quiet, health-giving watering place, prettily situated at the foot of the Downs, possessing a tonic air, beautiful scenery, and perfect restfulness ... Seaford does not desire a pier nor a fashionable parade, but it has one of the finest stretches of seafront in the kingdom, wholly given up to visitors.[17]

Apart from quiet and health, what had Seaford to offer to its late Victorian visitor? Although its virtues were rarely trumpeted abroad – its first guide book did not appear until 1904 – it had a choice of modest activities, which can be tracked down in the few remaining files of the short-lived *Seaford and Newhaven Gazette*. Seaford's season began at the end of May when the paper published the first list of visitors. They shared the thirty or so lodging-houses – four or five people each at the start of the season – small hotels and houses-to-rent, provided by the Seaford Bay Estate Company for such people as they wanted to attract. For entertainment, there was the promenade, almost two miles long, where the council built a couple of shelters in the 1890s and the Volunteer Band performed regularly. That apart, the visitors joined in the modest entertainments of the townsfolk. The *Albert Hall* was the main centre of activity, well away from the sea, the venue of Sunday schools, Liberal Club smokers and concert-parties. Here minor travelling troupes performed, but the bulk of entertainment was locally-made – farces, concerts, recitals, put on by the town's worthies and their wives and daughters. The visitor to Seaford was not provided for distinctively as a holiday-maker, but shared in the type of activity he was equally likely to find at home in suburban London. When an element of vulgar commercialism appeared it was removed, in one case forcibly, by the developer's men. Some residents complained about this high-handed action.

> How much of Seaford belongs to the people of Seaford? and how much to the Bay Estate Company? It is a question that is being asked every day in Seaford, the inhabitants of which contend that their rights have been ruthlessly swept away in many instances by the Company![18]

A troupe of Pierrots had been ejected from their stand on the front in September 1894 by the Bay Estate Company's agent and twenty men, who forcibly carried off the piano and left it in a side street. The agent said many residents had complained about the nature of the songs. Another more serious conflict made plain the economic and social implications of the town's determination to cater for respectable visitors and quiet residents. Good golf courses on the Head were Seaford's greatest attraction for the better-off holiday-maker, and an issue arose over a suggestion that Sunday play should be allowed. Robert Lambe, another of Seaford's developers, argued:

> We don't want that class of men here who would play golf on Sundays, and, as a tradesman said to me the other day, a man who would play golf on Sunday would not be particular whether he paid his debts or not![19]

The question was thrashed over for a year, in the press, in the council, the churches, chapels, Pleasant Sunday Afternoons and Seaford Mutual Improvement Society. The golf club eventually bowed to pressure and stayed shut on Sundays.

The land holding pattern of a resort was an important factor in determining its progress, especially from the point of view of its 'social tone'. A large landowner was in a position to enforce covenants on householders, which could maintain the respectability of a town, either in its appearance or in its decent residential character. Professor Perkin has pointed to the contrast in the North West between the high social tone of Southport, where the land was split between two families, and unrespectable Blackpool, whose land was held in fragmented small units without the control of a dominant landlord.[20] There are some snags to this theory even as it applies to the North West. Blackpool itself had a respectable quarter in the north of the town; Fleetwood never achieved in social terms what the Fleetwood-Hesketh family had hoped for; and Grange-over-Sands gained a reputation for high social tone without being dominated by a monopoly landowner. However, the effective exercise of landed power by the Bay Estate Company at Seaford in order to clean up the beach seems to suggest that Professor Perkin's theory is applicable to Sussex, as does respectable Eastbourne under the improving unitary ownership of the 7th Duke of Devonshire. On the other hand, no less respectable than either Seaford or Eastbourne was Worthing, a town with a fragmented pattern of ownership, and, by the same token, Bungalow Town on Shoreham Beach was a unitary development on a single estate which fell far short of contemporary notions of respectability, at least as far as the life style of its occupants was concerned. The study of Brighton in the second half of the nineteenth century introduces a further element into the analysis, because, whereas Brighton was a large leasehold town with a fragmented pattern of land ownership, the power of pressure groups and the political process ensured important victories for the forces of respectability during the 1880s and the 1900s.

In Seaford the seasonal pattern of holiday-making was simple – the visitors came for a brief period in the summer, and in the winter there was a long break. At Brighton, however, it was claimed in 1870 that 'except

41

from January to May, there is always some kind of season'.[21] A variety of visitors filled the different seasons of the year. The excursionists came in July and August, the visitor to the fashionable Season in the autumn and the family holiday-maker in the spring and late summer. By separating the visitors into individual seasons as well as distributing them through different parts of the town Brighton hoped to avoid friction amongst the rival holiday factions. Nonetheless, the town suffered the onset of a decline in its holiday business during the 1880s. The social deterioration of the fashionable Season has already been referred to and, just as Brighton was a reluctant host to the tripper, so she proved an ineffective one to the resident holiday-maker. In a sense the town had simply become too big effectively to cater for the cosy holidays 'away from it all' that were then the vogue, especially at a competitive price. Trade was lost to rivals far and near, from Biarritz to Bognor and the lodging-houses declined in number quite rapidly after the 1880s. 1886, for example, was a 'bad season not accounted for by the weather and the drains'[22] and the local press commented on the derelict air of the town, especially the empty lodging-houses.

From the mid-nineteenth century Brighton's economic life diversified in several new directions. The provision of residential and regional services became important to the town as did education – there were seventy schools in the 1860s – and when the railway workshop was established in the 1850s it became a centre of manufacture. There was also the myriad of small workshops producing clothing, furniture and the other locally-manufactured goods typical of any large Victorian community. Consequently the holiday trade was no longer the sole source of prosperity for Brighton and a conflict of interest developed between the permanent residents and the special requirements of the holiday visitor. During the 1860s, for example, Brighton was divided over the sewer question between those who wished to have them reconstructed, scared of what the summer smell might do to the visitors, and those who thought that such an expensive scheme would bring no benefit at all to the permanent residents in the town. Numerous schemes were proposed for revitalising Brighton's ailing holiday industry during the crucial decade of the 1880s, yet strong hostility from residents and from established enterprises fearing new competition combined to defeat nearly all the proposals. The Town Council, on the whole, sided with a residential lobby and seems in 1884, indeed, to have marshalled such vested interests as the West Pier, the Chain Pier and the Corporation-owned *Aquarium* in successful opposition to a proposal to build a new Central Pier at the foot of West Street. The same alliance failed to stop the Palace Pier Bill in 1888, but many similar schemes foundered on local hostility, the Brighton *Eiffel Tower* of 1891, the Hove *Winter Garden* in 1882 and the Brighton *Winter Garden* in 1892, for example.

During the 1900s the Council found itself on the other side in this tussle. The holiday trade was again in the doldrums, but there was a new touch of realism about the *Brighton Gazette*'s suggestion in 1904 that since 'the classes have deserted Brighton . . . we must now cater for our new clients'.[23] Previously, this would have meant rough recreations, but now there was much less of a threat to the social order coming from this source. Indeed, fundamental anxieties on that score had

43

already been largely allayed during the 1880s. There was also a lesson to learn from the North. G. R. Sims, writing in the *Referee*, blamed drunkenness among south coast trippers on early closing and poor entertainment facilities. Blackpool and Douglas successfully dealt with the problem by catering more effectively for the tripper with 'palm palaces and dance halls' and entertainments open until midnight.[24] Accordingly, in 1908 Brighton Corporation in conjunction with Joe Lyons the caterer and William Forbes the general manager of the London Brighton and South Coast Railway devised a major entertainment scheme, a *Summer and Winter Palace* to be built on the foreshore at the west end of the town. The Corporation was to act as landlord and it proved to be a highly controversial project. The *Brighton Gazette* welcomed the *Palace* at first as a sign of a new attitude to enterprise in the town.

> The record well shows that the policy of frowning upon strangers and of doing little ourselves to make Brighton attractive was responsible for the depression which began to be felt in the year 1891. . . . That spirit of antagonism is entirely changed on the present occasion, and personally, I regard that as one of the best omens of the future of Brighton.[25]

The Railway Company had an overt interest in the scheme but, despite fears that it might cheapen the class of traffic coming to Brighton, the *Gazette* supported the proposal.

> . . . the Palace will fill our lodging houses. . . . We have never had anything corresponding to the ambitiousness of the design and if we reject it, the opportunity is not likely to recur.[26]

At a meeting of the General Purposes Committee of the Town Council, however, Councillor Broadbridge, a strong supporter of the scheme, mentioned the possibility of compensation being paid to the private backers in the event of failure. This news spread immediate alarm amongst the ratepayers, many of whom could remember the unexpected costs incurred as a result of the Corporation's previous purchase of the *Aquarium*. Public meetings were held where suspicions were raised by the Corporation's refusal to produce a model of the scheme. A resolution, framed by Sir Henry Kimber M.P., Chairman of the *Bedford Hotel*, was sent to the Council.

> . . . that, in the opinion of this meeting the Town Council holds the foreshore for the benefit of the inhabitants at large and that they are not justified in permitting the appropriation of any of it by a private company to the serious financial detriment of individual ratepayers owning property fronting the proposed casino, and to the enforced limitation of the use of the foreshore by the inhabitants generally.[27]

The lodging-house proprietors, on the whole, backed the scheme, whilst the hoteliers, especially those whose frontages would be blocked by the *Palace*, opposed it. 'Smart residents' from the Sassoons to Lord Hamilton combined with the ratepayers groups to apply pressure on the Council, now divided on the matter. The preparation of the necessary Parliamentary Bill continued right up to the last moment in November 1908, when Lyons and Forbes, dissatisfied with the details of the draft Bill, pulled out of the scheme. In an open letter to the town they wrote:

We have determined not to continue with the scheme during the forthcoming session. We are, moreover, influenced in coming to this decision by the fact that apparently a considerable number of Brightonians are opposed to the scheme and we certainly have no wish to attempt to force a scheme upon Brighton which does not meet with the general approval of the inhabitants.[28]

Thus, it was not the influence of a dominant, monopoly landlord but a pressure group of residents in alliance with the hoteliers who won this victory on behalf of the forces of respectability. By this time, the King was again in residence in Brighton and the 'classes' were into their fashionable Indian Summer. The *Gazette* now argued that good, outdoor music, popular aquatic fêtes, polo matches, lawn tennis tournaments and facilities for motor picnics were what the holiday visitor most wanted in Edwardian Brighton.

CHAPTER 3

DOMESTIC CONSUMPTION

The leisure class has always used private homes for recreational purposes. In Victorian and Edwardian times, however, growing affluence and the forces of emulation made it both possible and necessary for other sections of society to imitate this practice. This new development was also reinforced by the strong Victorian emphasis on family life as an important ingredient for respectability, especially in the context of recreation.

In the eighteenth century the social life of the gentry and aristocracy alternated between country estates and town houses, and high social position required the maintenance of large houses beyond the immediate living needs of a family. The *Quarterly Review* in 1828 described the responsibilities of a gentleman:

> ... the honourable condition of an English nobleman or country gentleman (was to reside) the greater part of the year on his estates; the centre of family connexions; opening his family mansion with munificent hospitality; preserving the attachment, encouraging the industry, and restraining the moral habits of his tenantry; performing the various local duties of a magistrate and citizen. ...[1]

Thus, family mansions were, in effect, 'open' houses, which were filled at periods of hospitality with regiments of friends, relatives and hangers-on, as well as a large number of servants. In the democratic town, supplementary use might be made of public assembly rooms for entertaining, but, beyond the sometimes quite modest private apartments of the family, country houses normally extended to 'public' reception rooms – dining, ball and drawing. Their scale reflected the status of their owners. Social movement upwards was marked by expensive restoration and extensions, downwards by dereliction or even sale to a wealthy newcomer.

In nineteenth-century Sussex there were many examples of town and country houses still within this 'public' tradition. There were also houses built in a different and newer tradition, designed for more private and secluded use. Each life style found exponents drawn both from the old landed families as well as from the *nouveaux riches*, who arrived in the county, flush with railway or speculative profits, bent on acquiring a place in the country. Two medieval buildings, both modernised during the nineteenth century, exemplify these two contrasted approaches to country-house living – *Battle Abbey* and *Arundel Castle*, the country seats of two dissimilar dukes.

Battle Abbey was the first of the two to be modernised and this was intended explicitly for private use. By the 1850s, the house and small gardens were in disrepair. Under the 'naughty' Sir Godfreys, 1800–1830, the Webster family had misspent substantial resources, and finally became heavily mortgaged in order to support unmarried female relatives and to pay off large accumulated debts. The house was beyond their means, and had to be sold in 1857 to Lord Harry Vane, later Duke of Cleveland, whose income came less from his local estates than from his extensive coal-ownership in County Durham. His

48

formidable Duchess's taste combined with the skills of Henry Clutton, the architect, to effect a transformation. As described in the Duchess's own *History of Battle Abbey*, this gives an insight into the private social habits and visual assumptions of one section of the leisured aristocracy.

'The terrace was at that time a woeful place enough; uneven, neglected and surrounded by the jagged fragments of the destroyed wall . . . (now it) may be called both our air-bath and our quarter-deck, for there are not many days in the year when it is not a pleasant walk . . . the view it commands is wide, and if it cannot be called beautiful, it is still full of variety and interest. . . . It is evening – the sweet Scottish 'gloaming' – that I like our upper terrace the best, when the west has received its baptism of fire, and the sun has sunk to rest in splendour, as a hero should die; 'So stirbt ein Held – Beneidungswerth!'[2]

To the Abbot's house was added a library wing in the Tudor style for the Duke's collection of books and Italian paintings, the booty of his Grand Tours. Perhaps, the best improvement was the clearing of the ruined crypt of the Abbey Church, a stagnant pond in Webster's day, and the laying out of the formal gardens which still exist today. For the Clevelands, Battle Abbey was not a great ducal mansion but a refuge from both public life in London, and the grime and class antagonism which surrounded their principal seat, *Raby*, in County Durham.

Arundel Castle, by contrast, was very much a public building – less a retreat than a dominant centre for the surrounding populace, the visible expression of the continuing local power of England's premier peer, the

Duke of Norfolk. The medieval ruins and a modest Georgian mansion were completely revamped by C. A. Buckler during the 1890s, in an anachronistic and 'unfeeling Windsor Castle style', as Pevsner puts it. It was paid for with the failing income of a late-Victorian agricultural estate, again supplemented by industrial holdings, this time the Duke's in Yorkshire.

Many of the great houses in the county, however, had to share in a recreational development which began to intrude on the privacy of their occupants, the practice of visiting 'stately homes'. The abundant topographies of the Georgian period had encouraged travellers to visit houses of note, but this had been a pastime largely for fellow owners and others likely to be treated as equals by the gentry. In the Victorian period, however, regular visiting days were instituted for the inquisitive middle classes, together with occasional day trips organised for 'respectable' workers, and especially their children. The motive for welcoming visitors was not at this stage the crumbling economy of great houses since charging for admission was unknown, although many owners tried to regulate their times of opening. Perhaps it was thought that submitting to public viewings of grand living was a social duty which might also produce feelings of respect. Where proud owners refused to undergo these inspections as in the West Midlands, for example, the poisoning of rural relations was the inevitable local consequence.

A great stimulus for country-house visits was given both by the growth of country railways and by the publication of cheap guide books to the principal resorts, containing selected excursions to the rural hinterland. Even Battle Abbey's privacy was disturbed as the house became an object for new pilgrimages from Hastings. The Duchess wrote her own description of this development.

> No account of Battle Abbey could be considered complete without some mention of the visitors that hold a triumphal jubilee there on every Tuesday throughout the year. They are most numerous in the summer months, when the London shopkeepers take their annual holiday by the seaside. . . . But they come in all seasons, and I may add, in all weathers. The local newspapers urge the excursion as an indispensable duty, and they are only too glad to have something to do and somewhere to go. . . . The favourite excursion was into the park; not, I am sorry to say, with any idea of examining the field of battle, but simply to eat and drink. Here the hampers were unpacked, and joyous picnic parties formed circles around them on the turf, making merry – always noisily, and sometimes obstreperously. . . . I still occasionally hit upon depots of empty soda water bottles, snugly stowed away in the shrubberies like eggs in a nest.[5]

The Duchess tried limiting the number of free tickets, introducing guides and noticeboards to restricted areas. Yet, still the visitors came, eight hundred or more on a fine afternoon, and there was no mention of any attempt at closure. This development, however, was restricted to those houses reached by the railway system and a great many Sussex houses only received the occasional antiquarian visitor, until the charabanc and financial pressures after the First World War removed their final defences.

An example of the *nouveau riche* house designed for 'public' living was *Normanhurst*, near Battle, erected in 1867 for Thomas Brassey, one of the three sons of the railway contractor, and since demolished. The parvenu

51

father was even accepted into the world of the Duchess of Cleveland herself, more, it must be said, for his prudent Victorian virtues than for his opulence. In her own words:

> Beginning life, as he was fond of boasting, behind a wheelbarrow, he ended by bequeathing his sons six millions of money, and what, in these days of reckless speculation, is the rarer legacy of a stainless name. His was ever unsurpassed for honour and integrity.[3]

'Integrity' brought for the Brassey family a fortune, acceptance and an ostentatious house in the French *chateaux* style by Habershon, Brock and Webb. The Duchess sardonically described,

> . . . the new man in his new house, surrounded by new plantations, in the midst of grounds treeless but for them, as if to prove how slowly, at whatever expenditure of money, a place can be created. But the situation is good, the view fine, and time alone is needed for its improvement.[4]

The owners of such houses often went to great lengths to emulate the older, gentry-style of country living. Their presence undoubtedly helped to revive and preserve country recreations, most notably in the new lease on life given to Sussex hunting by their support in the second half of the nineteenth century. Brassey's family also accepted the public responsibilities of landed incumbency by supporting local charities and erecting public buildings for 'improving' the poor, especially in Hastings.

During the last quarter of the century, there was a new wave of country-house building deep in the Weald.

The extension of the railway system meant that this remote countryside became more accessible from London and the combination of convenient transport and rural seclusion fulfilled to perfection the city dweller's ideal of private country-house living. During the 1880s, for example, the Sackville Estate near East Grinstead was dismembered for building plots as one of several speculative developments in the area.

> To Gentlemen desirous of Building for their own occupation, this Estate offers advantages rarely to be met with in such favourable combination, viz: Pure bracing air, beautiful scenery, pleasant drives and walks, near proximity and good access to London, also to the favourable watering-places of Brighton, Tunbridge Wells and Eastbourne.[6]

This new style of rural leisure shunned the public responsibilities entailed in owning large country estates, whilst small landscaped gardens served as adequate guards of privacy. Many of the houses were intended solely for use at weekends, and so were well provided with bedrooms and recreation rooms – billiards and smoking. They also served as symbols of the wealth, together with the nannies, croquet lawns and motor cars, that modest affluence could bring to City men. Some of the new houses were designed by noted architects, such as Norman Shaw, who was responsible for *Wispers* and *Standen,* whilst others were built by local men. The new 'Wealden Vernacular' style with its emphasis on prominent brick chimneys, hung tiles and secluded garden settings, deriving inspiration from older houses in the district, was popular for these new leisure houses. Indeed, these cosy retreats in the Weald were so successful that they created a lasting prototype for suburban housing, which is still evident today.

The country house was modified according to the scale and affluence of the new owners. Even the modest 'bungalow' came to Sussex as early as the 1870s, with estates for permanent residence around East Grinstead, followed by the spread of coastal 'holiday-homes'. The word 'bungalow', originally meaning a house of any type (even two-storeyed) for living the simple leisured life, as well as the building type, a single-storeyed structure with verandah and pyramidal roof, were both imported from India. One unusual and cheap source of 'bungalows' was discarded railway carriages, which were delivered by the railway company to the nearest station at £30 a pair. They were then towed into position, and even ferried across water, as at Shoreham Harbour. Local jobbing builders and site agents then took over and joined them in pairs or triplets to create new communities of small leisure homes at inland sites, as well as at points on the coast.

Domestic leisure was developed most quickly in the second half of the nineteenth century as a result of house-building for the middling classes, both lower and upper, working and retired. While few of the market towns escaped at least one row of villas, the larger towns obviously received most of them. A great concentration of villas was erected also in the new town of Hove, where the rapid speculative development of Cliftonville in the 1850s set the tone for the later expansion. By contrast, there was an anachronistic attempt in the streets around Grand Avenue, Hove, to provide a late Victorian version of Brighton's aristocratic Kemp Town, with its squares and terraces of houses for occupation during the fashionable season, but this proved a failure.

The future lay with individual homes. Built for families who could only dream of a country-house life style, most private houses of this type indulged fantasies of rural grandeur. Elaborate gardens to the larger villas were ingeniously worked to create within a quarter of an acre the illusion of a country estate, and so provide the privacy for enjoying country pleasures and open-air sports, lawn tennis, for example. Similarly, the building of specialised rooms for leisure pursuits, from the billiard and smoking rooms of the rich to the parlours and domestic shrines of the thrifty, was not only an indication of the new distinction between leisure and the other phases of life in the minds of their occupants, but also an essential aid to the development of domestic recreation. In advertising even the smaller houses, estate agents always emphasised the specialised recreation or 'reception rooms', shrunk as they often were to relatively cramped dining rooms and parlours.

The wealthier families ostentatiously overemployed servants to remove the slightest suspicion that the women of the house might ever lose a moment of leisure, so that in serviced families the greatest recreational opportunities went to women. When good servants became scarce after the 1880s, the development of labour-saving devices in the home served more to increase the leisure of servants than that of housewives, who themselves often had to learn housework for the first time. Of course, some types of recreation could only be found outside the home. It might be a visit to church or chapel, attendance at a secular society, a concert, or in fine weather, a healthy walk, maybe in the cemetery on Sunday afternoon, to see and be seen by neighbours whose approbation mattered. That apart, 'carriage folk', and their imitators, stayed respectably behind the hedges and walls of home. There was not even a tradition of eating-out apart from clubs for men and lunch bars later in the century. In nineteenth-century France, the bourgeoisie imitated in a flourishing restaurant-culture the *haute cuisine* that had been a mark of the best life the aristocracy had enjoyed under the *ancien regime*. In England, by contrast, the corresponding class learnt from its social superiors how to play games, sow lawns and carve its overcooked Sunday joints.

The recreational details and leisure expectations of life within a Victorian suburban home perhaps come most vividly to life from pages of household magazines and from advertisements of contemporary stores selling household goods. The indoor life of the 'suburbans' is often represented in Victorian fiction, but rarely, apart from numerous magazines of prudent housekeeping, in convincing factual accounts. The tendency of novelists to denigrate the unbending rigidity of that respectable life also overlooks its more worthy features. Whilst it takes little imagination to doubt that most Victorians spent every evening around the piano, home-made entertainment was clearly important. Maude Robinson's perceptive memory of life in Saddlescombe, *A South Down Farm in the Sixties*, for example, describes enthusiastic reading as the principal recreation, apart from the weekly Quaker meeting.

The facts about domestic life amongst the poorer classes are even more difficult to establish, but, given poor housing conditions, domestic recreation had little chance against the attractions of life outside the home. Leisure for the poor can rarely have been supported by the material enhancements of comfortable housing, although there was a chance of this in better housing, enjoyed where landlords carried out improvements. Indeed in this respect, the workers of rural Sussex may have been more fortunate than many of their urban contemporaries. The growing shortage of agricultural labour after the 1860s led to the rebuilding of estate housing, for example, that done by the Ashburnhams and on the Glynde estate. These newly-designed houses, however, rarely provided the specialised rooms for leisure which even a modest white-collar worker would have expected. In the towns, where houses were mostly built using the private leasehold system, plans for the separate use of rooms were often overriden by the pressure for multiple occupation by the poorer families. Slum clearance was begun by Brighton Council in the 1860s, but the rebuilding was left to private enterprise, and it was only in the 1890s that the Corporation itself began to build houses. The first examples were in St. Helens Road and May Road, opposite the Workhouse, now the General Hospital. The rents and the restrictions in letting, however, made even these houses the prerogative of respectable artisans, rather than of the poorest workers. Other councils in the county seem to have shunned house building, at least prior to 1909, when permissive legislation led to new developments, such as the terrace on Netherfield Hill at Battle.

Robert Tressell described the living room of a poor man, his wife and one child in a Hastings slum:

> This room was about twelve feet square and the ceiling, which was low and irregularly shaped, showing in places the formation of the roof – had been decorated by Owen with painted ornaments. . . . There were three or four chairs, and an

oblong table, covered with a clean tablecloth, set ready for tea. In the recess at the right of the fireplace – an ordinary open grate – were a number of shelves filled with a miscellaneous collection of books, most of which had been bought second-hand.[7]

Take away the books, for Owen was a socialist, and the scene might be typical. In general, however, it is difficult to see the home at the end of the century as the principal setting for the recreational activities of the very poor and in many cases, it proved second best to the attractions of other facilities outside the home, whether the street, the chapel or simply the corner pub.

CHAPTER 4

THE CORNER PUB

Alcoholic drink had been a normal feature of social life long before the nineteenth century. Most sports and games in the eighteenth century were accompanied by ample alcoholic refreshment, whilst abundant commercial premises, the inn and the ale-house, catered for casual drinking in public. Alcohol was also consumed in the home, especially on ceremonial occasions – harvest feasts, shearing rights or funeral wakes – when home-brews were often drunk. The rhythm of the agrarian year defined most of the seasonal reasons for festive drinking – on holy days, market-days and at fairs – but intermittent public events elections, for example were also used as excuses for further drinking-sprees. Various brews matched the different occasions, from the mild beer drunk by the gallon in the fields during warm weather, to the strong ale brewed for festive use.

During the nineteenth century, the combination of rising real wages, that is actual purchasing power, and the sustained growth in population, ensured that boom conditions for the drink-trade prevailed for most of the period. Although there were marked changes in the attitudes surrounding the supply of drink as well as in retailing methods, several traditional features persisted late into the century. At elections, for example, 'generous treating' was still used as a means of reinforcing older social and political bonds in the country districts. Horsham was a by-word for electoral corruption and the drunken scene at the election of 1847 was described in a contemporary account;

> All the . . . public houses had accounts, graduated according to their importance from the 'Black Horse', 'Richmond', 'Swan', 'Dog and Bacon', down to the little beershop on the extreme northern boundary of the parish, and nicknamed the 'Cold and Dirty'. . . . It is not too much to say that most of the male population of Horsham were frequently drunk, many were continually drunk, and some were continuously drunk, for the whole six weeks preceding election day; women too were frequently 'up the pole' with the men, and even some of the boys attending Collyer's School went to their lessons in a state of intoxication.[1]

Drink could be consumed in a variety of licensed premises. The inn, the beer-shop and the public house had been the principal suppliers in the eighteenth century, and they still dominated the trade in the following century. The different institutions could be identified by the choice of beverages and variety of other services on sale. Inns, such as the *Grenadier*, at Hailsham, sold the complete range of alcoholic drinks as well as overnight accommodation and food. By contrast, beer-houses were more humble institutions which sold beer exclusively. Normally run as a side-line by a landlord with another job, they offered meagre comforts to the poorer section of the community; in the countryside, indeed, only the labourers and never the farmers patronised them. 'Public houses' were the remaining institutions, the tavern and the ale-house. They sold a wider range of drinks, but did not provide rooms-to-let. Some were simple places, such as the *Foresters' Arms*, East Hoathly, and the *Cricketers' Arms*, Berwick, which was no more than a front room of a cottage. Others were elaborate buildings, subdivided into a series of differentiated bars. Most had a resident publican, but others were lock-up pubs, no less.

Gin-palaces emerged as a new attraction during the drink boom of the late 1820s. Their distinctive appearance was described in 1834:

> Instead of the compact and comportable look of the old ale house, open windows exhibiting part of the labouring community, carousing within at noon, or emitting the joyous chorus of an evening song; there's now a tasteless display of extravagant architecture over the whole exterior. The doors are studded with brass and the windows composed of splendid plates in ormolu frames, while the interior resembles a Grecian temple of former days. We've seen an arched lighted roof, supported on fluted Corinthian columns; Classic displays thickly sculptured on the walls, chandeliers of crystal and lamps of bronze suspended by richly gilt chains; and stately mirrors on all sides reflecting the mock grandeur of the scene.[2]

In plan they were typically one great room, without partitions, stripped of all comforts, even seats in some examples, and dominated by a single, large sales-bar. Gin-palaces in this strict sense were rare in Sussex, even in the resorts. As the century progressed, however, the term 'gin-palace' changed in meaning and came to be used to describe any lavishly decorated public house. These latterday 'gin-palaces' became a very important feature of the drink-trade in the county towards the end of the century.

The argument that licensed premises were exclusively concerned with the brutish function of selling alcoholic drink and nothing more, was a commonplace of temperance-literature which certainly received superficial confirmation from the story of the early gin-palaces. An article, entitled 'You Must Drink', in *All the Year Round* for January 1867, put it this way:

> Some years ago almost every public house had its parlour and tap room; the former devoted to social foregatherings of the neighbouring tradesmen, the latter provided with a fire and cooking utensils for the use of the labouring classes. The old-fashioned public house parlour was a scene of right pleasant social meetings after the labours of the day. Neighbours and cronies gathered together to discuss the affairs of the parish, or the politics of the nation, over a pipe or a pint or two of ale. And it was the landlord's pleasure to occupy the chair and play host and treat his customers as guests and friends. It's true that when customers were rather too long over their pints the waiter would come in and make a bungling pretence of stirring the fire or turning the gas up by way of a hint, but it was a hint and no-one was obliged to take it. But in the modern houses, however, the parlour and tap-room were done away with altogether, or converted into bars where the customer must come *like a bucket to a well* and fill himself and go away again. There are very few places for friendly gatherings and social converse left.[3]

The critics of drink regarded not only gin-palaces but also beer-houses as pernicious 'alcoholic wells'. The latter had increased greatly in number after the Act of 1830, which allowed anyone who paid poor rates to sell beer from his house on payment of two guineas to the Excise. In Sussex, local brewers even helped beer-houses proliferate by paying the licence fees of willing householders and in several instances, Ringmer and Icklesham, for example, they enabled premises to re-open which previously had been closed by reforming gentlemen. The rush to take advantage of this new free-dom provoked much criticism. The proponents of Poor Law Reform before 1834 argued that poor relief given in cash was often squandered at the local beer-houses, and, according to many Justices of the Peace, the Swing Riots of 1830 were also the direct result of the Beer-house Act. 'In my opinion', said the Vicar of Arundel, 'they arose from an increased profligacy, engendered in part by the system of beer-shops, the constant resort of the worst characters'. The inhabitants of Amberley 'congregated in the beer-shops, perusing malicious publications' and the authorities of Barcombe main-tained that, 'If some alteration does not take place in the beer-shops, there will not be an industrious man in the parish'.[4] It may be true that the provision of cheap drinking places tended to encourage indolence, vice and even insurrection among the rural poor. Yet wages in rural Sussex in the 1830s, nine shillings a week if you could get regular employment, were really insufficient for farm labourers often to indulge in excessive drink-ing. Later commentators were probably closer to the truth when they defended beer-houses as meagre centres of community-life, in areas where poor housing and poverty made family-life impossible and so beer-houses remained an important source of drink, both in the country districts and the towns, for the most of the century. Brighton still had about 270 of them in the 1890s, although they eventually faded in importance at the turn of the century, as a result both of the hostility of magistrates and strong competition from decent pubs and rival, non-alcoholic attractions.

The temperance theory of the 'bucket-and-well' im-perfectly describes the beer-house but it applies even less convincingly to the history of the inn and of the public house. Inns, for example, were the traditional setting for a wide variety of social events. On market days, they were the busy centre of commerce and unofficial banking. They were used for political discussions, and public meetings and for the consolidating dinners of protectionist farmers. Coroners' Inquests, tax gathering, even local government operated from inns. The *George*, at Battle, housed the Magistrates' Court until mid-century and was the scene of at least one minor affray, whilst the Battle Local Government Board, later the Urban District Council, held almost all its meetings in an upstairs room at the *George* until after the First World War.

The *Terminus*, in Seaford, was typical of a new type of small-town inn. It was a favourite place with the local workmen, as well as a resting place for the commercial travellers, following the opening of the railway in 1864. It was also where Seaford Liberals, Conservatives, Volunteer Corps and Friendly Societies held their annual dinners. Indeed, dinners had a traditional association with the older inns, where the entertainment of tenants on quarter days, and farmers' and political dinners had often taken place. This link was revived as enterprising landlords exerted themselves to attract trade from the many new clubs and associations of Victorian Seaford.

The older inns, however, lost an important part of their trade during the 1840s and 1850s, when the housing and feeding of travellers in the county was claimed by the railways. The motor car subsequently restored this trade to the inns in the twentieth century, but, meanwhile, the railways themselves had spawned a new breed of inn and, between 1840 and 1891, 52 new railway inns were built at Sussex stations and railway junctions, 35 *Railway Inns*, nine *Station Inns* and two *Locomotive Inns*. Minor imitations of the great railway-hotels, they housed the short-stay traveller as well as catering to the recreational needs of new communities, even of the railway workers themselves. The latter often lived in remote communities, such as at Northiam on the Kent-Sussex border, where, because the railway passed almost a mile outside the main village, the new *Railway Inn* became the dominant social centre of an isolated hamlet.

Apart from the inns, the public houses too fostered social activities as a supplement to drinking. The pub was often the principal meeting place in a district, sometimes the sole alternative, at least for the poor, to gathering out of doors, or in the church. Friendly Societies were associated with pubs, whose upper rooms also housed the meetings of trades unions and of other clubs and societies. The local Foresters as well as the Brighton Chess Club, for example, met in the *Unicorn*, North Street, Brighton. Publicans themselves organised sporting events, railway excursions and other entertainments, including football teams later in the century. Some pubs ran 'slate clubs' (savings clubs), and others held 'friendly leads' (informal concerts). Such improving activity, flourishing in the context of alcoholic drink, perplexed many temperance reformers.

The growing communities of manual and white-collar workers in the new housing estates of nineteenth-century Sussex presented a great commercial opportunity to the drink-trade, and the pubs were often the first communal facilities to be erected in the newly built estates. In Hove's Cliftonville, for instance, the

65

main developer, George Gallard, put a brewery at one end and a pub, the *Cliftonville Arms*, in the middle. The churches found it difficult to catch up with the breweries, unhindered as the latter were by the morass of law which attended the provision of any church or chapel. The religious authorities never really managed to make progress in this race, except on dry estates, where covenants forbade the sale of drink. In the 1890s, there were about 1,300 licensed premises in Sussex, or one for every 423 residents.

There is no simple answer to the question: 'Who used pubs?'. Drinking had its subtle social graduations, both within and between pubs. On Brighton's fashionable estates, for example, there were even specialist pubs catering for customers drawn exclusively from the superior class of servants. Contemporary surveys of drinking habits, usually coming from the pens of disapproving investigators of low life, could be misleading and the 'respectable' activities associated with inns and pubs complicate the picture of their use.

The geographical distribution of pubs and beer-houses in Brighton reveals one aspect of the picture. In the 1890s, with 300 pubs and 270 beer-houses, Brighton had one establishment for every 210 residents, a much denser provision than in the county as a whole. Surprisingly, however, it was not the areas most frequented by holiday visitors which had the greatest numbers of pubs. Admittedly, there was a high concentration round the station, but most of the pubs and beer-houses were in the back streets away from the seafront. The Carlton Hill area was especially noted for its numerous pubs – Edward Street had 26, Carlton Hill itself 14, and Upper Bedford Street 8 – but it was also one of the poorest areas in Brighton. Its residents included the casual workers and others in poorly-paid employment, and their intermittent pattern of work may explain the high incidence of pubs. To those whose work rarely filled a full day, let alone a complete week, the ever-open door of the beer-house was a standing invitation to drink.

The Victorian pub was not exclusively a male preserve. In Brighton, again, the pubs of the Church Road area were well-known stalking grounds for local prostitutes, but other women also visited pubs. Drinking in the middle of the day with female friends was popular, especially on Mondays, when some housekeeping money was left. Saturday night was also the time to visit the pub with husbands, and 'free and easies', the precursors of the Music Halls, were an attraction for the whole family on other nights of the week.

Drinking, more than any other recreation in Victorian England, attracted continuous criticism from the organised forces of respectability. John Burns described the comprehensive perils of the pub in a famous temperance verdict:

> The tavern throughout the centuries has been the antechamber to the workhouse, the chapel of ease to the asylum, the recruiting station for the hospital, the rendezvous of the gambler, the gathering ground for the jail.[5]

Bearing this message, the temperance and abstention movement spread throughout Sussex, but more into the large towns than the country areas, where the older drinking habits were less affected by changing attitudes and increasing prosperity. Those offsprings of church and chapel – the Independent Order of Rechabites (Salford Unity), the Order of the Sons of Temperance, the Independent Order of Good Templars, the Church of England Temperance Society and, above all, the Band of Hope Union – were all represented in the county. By the 1880s, the Church of England boasted 1,300 active abstainers in the Chichester diocese, but they were formally organised into groups only within 81 of its 300 parishes. One sceptic observed in 1860 that:

> Though the effect of these societies is laudable in the very highest degree, it cannot be dissembled that such an organisation is sadly too feeble to cope with the extensively ramified vice of intemperance.[6]

The extent of the 'vice' was shown by the fact that Brighton then supported 479 establishments supplying drink, the number of which was bitterly contrasted by the abstainers with the town's 519 food shops. Yet, even some of the Poor Law Guardians must have appreciated the nutritional value of beer for, as a temperance report pointed out, the Preston Union, near Brighton, spent more on beer for its 149 inmates in any one year than did 202 other unions with over 25,000 in their care; it amounted to 23s. 7d. per inmate per year.

The Band of Hope was established in Brighton in 1856, and its influence progressed first along the coast, and then inland to the small market-towns. Its principal target was children – they were easier to convert than their inebriate elders – and, by 1910, the Brighton branch was able to host the 42nd Annual Conference of the Band of Hope Union.

THE CAUSE OF TEMPERANCE in our own County will be strengthened by the excellent influence arising from the presence of so many leaders in the fight against Britain's direst foe.[7]

Temperance organisations further advanced their cause by employing political pressure, particularly during the Parliamentary elections of the 1880s. They also proselytised by developing their own peculiar leisure organisations, the Temperance Taverns, nineteen of them in Sussex at the end of the century, compared to 1,300 licensed premises. With the exception of those in Etchingham and Lewes, they were all in the coastal towns, aimed at the residents and modest family visitors alike. The *Hope of Brighton* Coffee Palace at 29 Duke Street, with its *Phoenix Hall* attached, was one example. In comparison with the casual companionship of the corner pub, however, the bad coffee and unsolicited preaching of the Temperance Tavern were poor attractions. As effective distractions from the pubs the Temperance Taverns were a failure, except as havens, like the churches, for women and children.

Despite the efforts of the temperance movement, the amount of alcoholic drink consumed by the average individual continued to rise until the 1870s. The highest official figure reached for beer consumption was 34 gallons a year for every man, woman and child reached in 1874, and for spirits one and a half gallons in 1875. The big spurt in money wages during the 1860s and early 1870s had encouraged this growing thirst, which consumed in cash terms 15 per cent of an average family's weekly expenditure. Since drink had always been an important item in the family budget, the rising real

69

wages of the nineteenth century had merely made it easier to indulge this traditional need for alcohol. Thus the the most effective enemy of the temperance movement was rising Victorian prosperity.

The average individual's intake of alcoholic drink, however, began to fall after the 1870s, more as a result of economic changes than of temperance warnings. For one thing, the relative price of beer began to rise. Although the money price of beer remained constant at $2\frac{1}{2}$d. a pint, the prices of many other commodities fell, including those of most foods. Also with the development of new commercial entertainments, such as professional football and the music hall, the drink-trade's virtual monopoly of the popular leisure market was lost to rival claimants on rising incomes, and consumers were further tempted away from drink by the increasing variety of new goods available in the shops – branded foods, off-the-peg clothing and even pianos.

Although the rising population in the period ensured that, despite the fall in individual consumption, the aggregate demand for beer continued to grow, the brewers were nevertheless frightened by these changes in consumer taste. The threat to their business was further accentuated by other new factors, the hostility to drink in the medical press, the growing political influence of temperance opinion, and the actions of local magistrates, who were adopting a much tougher line on the issuing of drink-licences. In reaction to this last development, the brewers began defending their position by securing for themselves possession of their retail-outlets, the pubs. In Sussex, the local brewers such as Harveys of Lewes, Halletts of Brighton and the Elm Brewery at Seaford each bought control over pubs in their own areas and, by 1890, 445 of the 588 licensed premises in Brighton itself had been integrated with breweries[8]. Meanwhile, the London brewers were interested in acquiring outlets for their beer in Sussex, especially on the coast, but their efforts were less successful and, at the turn of the century, 93 independent brewing firms were still operating in the county.

In order to raise the cash for buying up pubs many of the brewers went to the open money-market, first turning themselves into limited liability companies. By this action, the drink-trade also achieved a measure of financial respectability, particularly when clergymen could be persuaded to join the boards of the newly constituted companies, as happened in several cases. So successful was this policy that huge amounts of capital flowed into the industry in the 1880s and 1890s. A speculative boom in pub property was one consequence of this financial bonanza and brewers also took the opportunity to build new pubs and refurbish old ones, as a way of competing with the rival commercial entertainments, which were proliferating at the same time.

The pub decor, popularly regarded today as typically Victorian, dates basically from this period. An example of the late Victorian 'gin palace' was the *Royal Standard* in Queen's Road, Brighton, opened in 1899 to designs by H. W. Wakley and lavishly fitted with onyx, gilded plaster, silvered, bevelled and fluted glass, rich red tiles, French lincrusta and mahogany panels. The *Licensed Victuallers' Gazette* thought the *Royal Standard* was a highly efficient machine for selling drink to Brighton's visitors as they walked down Queen's Road to the sea, which 'foot for foot on superficial area . . . affords more accommodation for working a hurried passing trade than any other house on the coast. . . .'⁹

Another example of the new type of pub in Brighton was the *Seven Stars* in Ship Street, also converted in 1894. It was financed and managed by Ike de Costa, a well-known figure in the racing world, who had tried, implausibly and unsuccessfully, to introduce English betting to America and to popularise American trotting in England. In Brighton, he ran a sporting club, financed the Empire Music Hall and contributed to healthy, competitive and respectable athletics as Chairman of the Brill's Bath Swimming Club. Apart from its 'cosy corners and bright radiant elegance', the *Seven Stars* received 'Central News telegrammes' throughout the day and all the 'professional papers', and kept a smoking and concert room upstairs, which was 'in constant request for football gatherings and buffalo lodges.'

Such 'gin-palaces', however, halted only temporarily the relative decline of the drink trade, and even the 'reform pubs' of the subsequent decade faired no better, despite the children's rooms, coffee services and neo-Georgian exteriors which the Kemp Town brewery introduced to Brighton during the 1920s and 1930s. Except in some of the new suburbs the property developments of brewers also were cut back during the first decade of the century, largely as a result of the economic difficulties caused by the onset of the long-term fall in aggregate beer production. The arsenic scare of 1900 had played a part in this, as well as the stagnation in real wages which persisted throughout the 1900s. In these economic circumstances, people cut down their consumption of alcoholic drink rather than its attractive alternatives, the taste for which had been firmly established in the previous two decades of economic change. Nonetheless, by 1911, the average family was still spending as much as nine per cent of its weekly expenditure on drink, and hence the corner pub retained its Victorian pre-eminence as the main supplier of commercial recreation to Edwardian Sussex.

CHAPTER 5

FOR YOUR ENTERTAINMENT

The people of Lewes were offered (on 11 September 1851), at the Assembly Rooms of the *Star Hotel* the following tempting theatrical entertainment:

> Mr. Albert Smith has the honour to announce . . . that he will give his new Literary, Pictorial and Musical Entertainment . . . THE OVERLAND MAIL . . . Stalls 4s., family ditto 10s. 6d. . . . unreserved seats 1s. . . . Evening dress will be observed in the stalls.[1]

This type of presentation, the Victorian embodiment of the travelling player tradition, was typical of the occasional incursion of commercial culture into the small world of the market towns of Sussex. Mr. Albert Smith also presented during this particular visit to Lewes:

> Professor Parker, the celebrated swordsman . . . (who) will have the assistance of professors Quick and Sutton from Brighton, and Sergeant Johnson, late of the 14th Light Dragoons. The attraction of the evening will further be enhanced by the appearance of two gentlemen amateurs from Hastings, who are also no mean adepts in the use of the broadsword. It may be well to observe that Professor Parker was the winner of the Gold Medal at the Scotish (sic) fetes in Holland Park this summer. . . . Her Majesty is almost invariably attendant . . . the entertainment given by Professor Parker appears to be quite as attractive to the fair as to the sterner sex; and as the utmost care is taken to exclude anything that could be in the

slightest degree objectionable, these *Assaults d'Armes* are largely patronised by the families of the highest classes.

In the same week, another travelling variety show of an even more bizarre kind could be sampled at Hastings.

GREAT NOVELTY, the BOSJEMANS or AFRICAN SAVAGES, also the Juvenile Harpists, the Lockwood family.

The 'great novelty' took the form of an anthropological lecture with a hunt mimed on stage by pygmies. The Juvenile Harpists played 'Prince Albert's March' and 'the Harpists' Tour of Scotland'. These itinerant shows remained a basic ingredient of professional entertainment in Sussex until the era of the First World War, especially in the areas outside the coastal towns. As the nineteenth century progressed, however, new theatrical entertainments and enterprises appeared, which sought to exploit the ever more varied and specialised tastes of the expanding and prospering populations in the towns. Not that the travelling shows had all been by any means cheap. The top price for the 'Overland Mail' was 4s. and the bottom price for both this show and the 'Bosjemans' was also not cheap at 1s. These prices, indeed, meant that only the well-heeled or the thrifty could afford to attend and the same was true of the level of prices at the principal permanent theatres in Sussex, the three *Theatres Royal* in Brighton, Worthing and Chichester, which maintained the eighteenth-century tradition of play-houses in the county.

In their early days, at the end of the eighteenth century, these theatres had depended on the patronage of the local gentry, the visiting aristocracy and the officers from the garrisons of the Napoleonic Wars, and so Brighton's fall from fashionable favour during the 1830s affected their fortunes badly. Accordingly, a brisk turnover took place in the leases of all three theatres and the *Theatre Royal* at Worthing was actually closed for several seasons in the decade of the 1840s. In the end, not even the patronage of the Dukes of Richmond and Norfolk during the 1850s could save the theatres in Worthing and Chichester. The *Theatre Royal* at Chichester finally closed in 1859 when entertainment shifted to the Assembly Rooms, and even Henry Nye (later Nye Chart, who made the fortunes of the *Theatre Royal* at Brighton) was unable to save Worthing's theatre after obtaining its lease in 1853.

> The pit was occupied by three fishmen and a little girl stretched asleep on one of the benches; three bereaved looking gentlemen appeared sufficiently impressed with the loneliness of their position in the upper boxes; a score of lively lads in the gallery by their noise, made the desolation more apparent.[2]

It too was closed for good in 1855.

The larger the town the easier it was to experiment with programmes and adapt them to the changing tastes of the new clientele. During these crucial years, therefore, the *Theatre Royal* at Brighton continued to attract sufficient audiences to ensure its survival.

> From 1830 to 1860 was the palmy time of the melodramas and perhaps at no provincial theatre did they flourish more than at the Brighton one. Perhaps the construction of the edifice itself had something to do with this. The gallery in which the 'gods' did congregate was of disproportionate size to the other parts of the building. It extended much farther back than that in the

present theatre (1891) (erected in the lesseeship of Mr. H. N. Chart) and accommodated 700 to 800 persons. As may be supposed, the taste of so large a portion of the audience had to be consulted, and that taste inclined decidedly to the melodrama, and the more sensational the better. The playbill was consequently divided into two portions; the first being intended for the boxes and the pit, and the latter for the gallery; and to make the division more marked, it was at nine o'clock when the first half of the performance was got through, and when a good many of the occupants of the boxes took their departure, that the half-price were admitted – the gallery at 6d. and, accordingly, not a very refined class. There was no mistaking their entrance, it was like a torrent of feet and voices, as they rushed with hooting and halloing and whistling from the back to the front seats.[3]

This 'rough' audience came to see such fare as *The Wood Demon, Frankenstein, Agnes or the Bleeding Nun of Lindberg* and *The Wife of Seven Husbands*, but, after the 1860s, Nye Chart set out to attract a 'better class of person' to the *Theatre Royal*. He therefore rebuilt the theatre to designs by Phipps, reduced the amount of low-price accommodation and raised the other prices, with the result that the proportions of rich and poor in the audience changed and an altogether more 'respectable' audience moved in. The new matinee audiences of the 1880s reinforced this improving trend. As for the productions, the provincial touring companies were replaced by London companies who presented straight drama. It was the beginning of the present Brighton practice of hardy favourites mixed with previews of West End performances. The raising of theatrical standards was also the result of the competition Chart faced in the 1890s from the other four theatres in the town and the pier companies, which even turned to grand opera in 1911! 'London style and London finish', as one commentator put it, matched the plutocratic element already noted in Brighton's hotels at the century's end, although the high social tone relaxed a little under the subsequent management of H. Cecil Beryl.

> . . . evening dress is no longer *de rigueur* in the stalls and boxes of the Royal, even in the height of the smart season . . . (there was) the incongruous spectacle of a gentleman in rough tweeds . . . the freedom of life that prevails in Brighton has inured them to shocks of this kind.[4]

The *Royal* remained the principal theatre for straight drama in Sussex. Other theatres concentrated on melodrama, or mixed programmes of drama interspersed with 'variety'. These minor 'mixtures' were an important element in the theatrical entertainment of late Victorian England, and their character can be judged from a review of a performance at the *Hippodrome*, Brighton, in 1911.

> In appearing in a sketch called *The Bridge*, Mrs Patrick Campbell has clearly realised the type of work that appeals to a varied audience. *The Bridge* is a piece of concentrated melodrama of a well-exploited type . . . the curtain has hardly fallen on Mrs. Patrick Campbell before Phil Ray is on the platform, with his paint-distended mouth, his 'dickey' worn outside, and his mocking of the actress's last words. *The Bridge* does not put one into the frame of mind to enjoy the jokes of the man distending what a doctor calls his abdomen and expatiating on the amount of beer that it holds.[5]

Such mixed fare fully satisfied neither the respectable not the rough elements in the audiences. The former found more to suit its dramatic tastes in the early music halls and their precursors, the 'Free and Easies' of the large public houses. Brighton's *Canterbury Hall* in Church Street, 'a locality not by any means remarkable for its respectability', was a mixed example, both socially and theatrically. A good description of it came from 'A Graduate of the University of London' in 1861.

(It) is a considerable improvement upon the other dirty public houses with which this portion is infested. . . . In front of the stage, in a stall higher than the rest, is a place set apart for the chairman, as we suppose he is called, a dark young man with his hair parted in the middle, and who, we cannot help thinking, might be more profitably and honourably employed than in sitting here night after night smoking cigars and drinking from seven till twelve o'clock. He looks rather pale, and well he may be, for the room is full of tobacco smoke, and his work itself must be rather dull, not such as sends the blood gaily through the veins. The majority of the people around us are evidently respectable, consisting for the most part of small tradesmen and their families. Here and there you see a shop assistant, or a few clerks and school assistants, with an occasional contribution from 'My Lords' kitchen in the shape of a be-buttoned footman or a well-fed coachman, rejoicing in the faultless quality of his plush.[6]

To mix with the 'better' company cost 6d. whilst the rest of the places, priced 3d., were filled with 'operatives in their work-a-day clothes . . . old men and women . . . young mothers with barefoot, ill-clad children. . . . We condemn it because we believe that the association of drinking with public amusement is pernicious in the highest degree, being a refined method of drawing the young into unsteady and idle habits.' Yet, this was a fairly innocuous pleasure palace. There were no obscenities, no overt drunkenness and only one point of 'immorality' stood out. The hall was a well-known parade ground and pick-up point for the prostitutes of Brighton, which, beyond a series of guesses at their number, and a list of the well known 97 'bad houses' of the mid Victorian town, is all that is known about the local 'nymphs of the pave'.

Canterbury Hall and the other pubs used local, amateur acts, supplemented occasionally by magicians, singers and comedians from the ranks of the professional, itinerant entertainers. They went on providing this kind of entertainment until harassed by magistrates later in the century. The new tendency, however, was for the development of purely professional music-hall theatres, distinct from pubs, with the stress on the show rather than the drink. The *Empire*, the *Oxford* and the *Alhambra* were early examples of this new genre in Brighton, but, perhaps the most attractive building was the *Hippodrome*, redesigned for Moss Empires, by Frank Matcham in 1901. Another building, also called *Hippodrome*, had previously operated as an indoor circus for many years in the north of Brighton. Its owner, Fred Ginnett, struggled for fourteen years to obtain a theatre licence against the campaigns of the entrenched Nye Chart. Ginnett's aim was to supply 'rational entertainment (to the) 20,000 people in the north of the town who could not afford 6d. for a stage play'. By 1890, Ginnett and Chart had worked out a *modus vivendi*, but in its first year the *Hippodrome*, newly-named *Gaiety*, tried to go 'respectable', and priced the seats from 6d. to £1. It failed to attract the people for whom it was intended and soon became the seediest meeting place in the town, at least of those where admission fees were charged. When eventually Evans

81

and Dunkin, already owners of the *Eden* and *Empire*, bought the *Gaiety* in 1898, the expenditure needed to save the theatre broke them.

Melodramatic as the basic fare of the poorest theatres was, it served to explore in simple terms the standard moralities of late Victorian England. In the *Gaiety*, where the songs often carried an element of diluted social criticism, there was no simple message of social acceptance, but, as the Boer War loomed and the fear of Germany increased, the songs and spectacles became increasingly jingoistic. Furthermore, audiences by then had also shown that they preferred more sophisticated and pricey spectacles. This attracted the energies of ambitious impresarios new to the theatrical business who sought to corner all the top artists and tour expensive shows on nationwide circuits. In this way, the mass-entertainment industry began to emerge, with its palatable messages delivered by 'classless' artists of the widest possible commercial appeal to the respectable audiences which flocked to see them.

Meanwhile, Ginnett had built another theatre in North Road, Brighton, where he put on spectacular illusions – for 4d. you could see *The Streets of London* and *The Poor of New York* which included a 'Great Fire Scene' in Act V, under the direction of the Hove Firemen. This theatre was soon renamed the *Grand* and, for a time, rivalled the *Theatre Royal* in the quality and character of its presentations. In 1904, however, it was incorporated into the local Empire and Eden Syndicate and returned to housing variety-shows.

At the same time as professional entertainment developed, the wealthier classes were discovering the delights of taking part themselves in amateur dramatics.

The Brighton Green Room Club, 'Aristocratic Amateurs', founded in 1887, was an example of an amateur group and it specialised in performances of light comedies for presentation at the Hove Town Hall. Many clubs came into prominence in the 1890s, as meeting places for the leisured and unattached young, and they became the winter alternative to the cycling and lawn tennis clubs of summer. They could be found not only around the leafier suburbs of the coastal towns, but also in the market towns. Ample multi-purpose proprietary halls were built to supplement the church halls and they provided suitable venues for such theatrical activities. In presenting the plays of Oscar Wilde, for example, and many lesser farces, these clubs brought together in leisured solidarity people of similar social class. 'Many of the elite of Seaford and Blatchington' saw a local councillor and a local doctor, J. F. Farncombe and Dr. Morgan, act together in *Arthur Onslow*, in June 1894, at the local *Albert Hall*, as part of a regular series of amateur productions.

On 5 March 1900, in the sixth month of the Boer War, the last act in the *Alhambra*'s variety show was advertised as:

> The Edison-Thomas Royal Vitascope with an extensive selection of subjects connected with the present crisis, including Embarkation of the Troops . . . and the arrival of Lord Roberts at Cape Town.[7]

During the following ten years, the new cinema-shows caught on very quickly, being mainly slotted into the programmes of the existing music halls. In January 1911, for example, the *Hippodrome* showed an 'animated picture' of the siege of Sydney Street.

> One is able to see the shadowy form of the doomed house. . . .
> With a little imagination one can picture at least the possi-
> bility of the maddened desperadoes struggling for life behind
> that moving pall.[8]

On 3 June 1911, however, the *Academy Picture Palace*
opened in West Street, Brighton, as an early example of
purpose-built cinema. During its first week, the *Academy*
showed programmes of delayed-interval pictures of
spring flowers, interspersed with newsreels, already
quite common and often hand-tinted. Both were accompanied by full orchestra. The Mayor was invited,
but could not attend the first night because by coinci-
dence he was opening the rebuilt theatre on the *Palace
Pier* that same evening. It was the deputy Mayor, therefore, who presided at the Picture Palace and thereby
honoured the inception of the boom-entertainment of
the inter-war period.

CHAPTER 6

SACRED HARMONIES

During the early nineteenth century music in Sussex, rather like the theatre, depended on an established tradition of aristocratic patronage. The development of Brighton and of the other lesser resorts as extensions of the London Season brought to the county the small orchestras and itinerant songstresses of assembly-room and drawing-room society. There was also the occasional visits of the musical darlings of international high society, such as Rossini, who sang in the *Royal Pavilion* in 1823, and Paganini, who played in the assembly room of the *Old Ship Hotel*, Brighton, during 1827.

With the decline of the area as an aristocratic centre, especially Brighton, it was left to the improving classes to maintain the tradition of concerts. Professional concerts were now organised in subscription series. The programmes often consisted of instrumental chamber music and included works by the leading composers of the day, European and British. In October and November 1853, for example, a series of three concerts took place at Brighton in the *Pavilion* on Mondays. The chamber music of Mozart and Beethoven formed the core of the programmes, but the final concert of the series contained the highlight 'when a Quartett of Mendelssohn, never before played in Brighton will be performed'.[1] The players were itinerant professionals, organised by William Kuhe, the central figure in the history of music in Brighton during the nineteenth century, and included Lazarus, a clarinettist from the Royal Italian Opera Covent Garden, who performed the Mozart *Clarinet Quintet*. Other concerts in 1853 were given by the 'Amateur Symphony Orchestra of 40 Players' and by two local singing teachers, Maria Coletti, a pupil of Mendelssohn, and Madame Sala. A German Band also played regularly in the *Pavilion* between 3 and 5 o'clock on Tuesdays, Thursdays and Saturdays, admission 6d.

November 1853 was also the occasion of a major, vocal event, four opera performances, presented at the *Theatre Royal* by Cramer, Beale and Co., who owned the 'Music Warehouse' in Brighton. Donizetti *Lucretia Borgia*, Bellini *Norma*, *I Puritani* Acts 2 and 3, *La Somnambula* Act 1 and *Huguenots* Act 1 were performed with an orchestra from the Royal Italian Opera and the ageing opera stars, Gossi and Mario. In general, however, the performance of large-scale works, especially those from the choral repertoire, was the responsibility of amateur societies, albeit using orchestras which were occasionally stiffened by local professional players. An important exception to this rule was the series of concert seasons organised between 1869 and 1883 by the celebrated Kuhe, a Czech pianist and music teacher, who had settled in London in 1847 and who kept a house at Brighton. The first of these 'Brighton Festivals' in 1869 consisted of 'fifteen grand subscription orchestral concerts on a scale never yet attempted in Brighton', held on consecutive days in Mr. Child's *Grand Concert Hall*, West Street. In the following year the Festival moved to the *Dome* where even more ambitious programmes of orchestral concerts and oratorios could be presented, Rossini *Stabat Mater*, Gounod *Gallia* and

Mendelssohn *Hymn of Praise*, for example. The enterprising Kuhe also used his Festival to encourage new talent, by commissioning new works and arranging first performances, which included *Lalla Rookh* by Frederick Clay, from which comes the song 'I'll sing thee songs of Araby'. Leading composers also visited Brighton for Kuhe's Festivals; Gounod, Costa, Benedict and Sullivan were amongst those who conducted their own compositions. But the Festivals lost money almost from the moment of their inception and, when the deficit reached £500 a season, a loss which had to be borne by the promoter, the project folded.

The cost of professional concerts with symphony orchestras, then as now, threatened so easily to exceed the receipts from ticket sales. It is therefore not surprising, especially after the decline in the number of private patrons living in the town, that requests for subsidies were eventually directed towards the Town Council. In pursuit of this end, unfavourable comparisons were frequently drawn between Brighton and the spas and resorts of Europe, most of which lavishly maintained their own orchestras. One result of this pressure was the decision in 1891 to put the finances of the Municipal Band on a regular basis, but the idea of a Municipal Orchestra was firmly resisted, although Bournemouth established the first permanent municipal orchestra in Britain in 1894. It was not deafness to music which kept the public purse in Brighton closed, but rather the belief that people valued and enjoyed most that which they paid for themselves. Perhaps, music too was regarded as less improving in its effect than other activities that had an equal claim on the rates.

In the 1900s the demand for a Municipal Orchestra

was linked to one for a Winter Garden which could at the same time house the orchestra and give botanical pleasure to the permanent residents of the town. The Council declined to build a Winter Garden since, it was argued, it had already acquired the *Aquarium* for this purpose some years previously and it was left to private enterprise to erect a new Winter Palace on the *Palace Pier*, which already possessed a concert hall suitable for 1,500 people, opened in 1901. But the Council could no longer resist the attraction of a Municipal Orchestra, which it agreed to subvent, starting in 1908. The first season was a success and the orchestra even played in *St. James' Hall*, London, under its regular conductor, Joseph Sainton. Brighton certainly got good value for money. There were concerts of popular classics twice daily, including Sundays, at the *Aquarium*, admission 6d., 3d, after 6.00 p.m. Further, there were more ambitious concerts at the *Dome* on Saturday afternoons with visiting *virtuosi*, admission 5s. reserved, 1s. unreserved. Annual uncertainty about the grant threatened the existence of the orchestra, but the Council decided to retain 40 players for the 1909 season.

In the same year the Council also lent support to Sainton in his efforts to inaugurate another series of Brighton Festivals, the second in the history of the town, an ambitious venture which involved an augmented version of the Municipal Orchestra. The first year, when amongst other events, Elgar conducted *The Dream of Gerontius*, was a great success, not least financially. Expenditure amounted to £958 and receipts were £8 in excess of this. The second Festival in 1910 was more ambitious than the first with 'full chorus and orchestra of 500 performers'. The Festival lasted four days and

1. BRIGHTON FROM THE WEST PIER

The conventional image of late Victorian leisure. Boaters and parasols shelter every face from the sun. *n.d., c. 1886.*

2. THE LAWNS, EASTBOURNE

This middle class resort had all the key attractions of a late Victorian/Edwardian seaside holiday. Natural beauty, up to Beachy. Head, solid boarding houses, bathing machines, a good crowd on the lawn, young ladies promenading in groups, respectable and summery. Note the large number of umbrellas/parasols in use – the air was good for the complexion, the sun not at all so. *c. 1900.*

3. SITTING ON THE CORNER

'We wunt be druv'. Apart from the pub, there was nowhere else for the agricultural labourer to go in his spare time – in bad weather only the 'living room'. The informal Sunday discussion, or village parliament, remained relatively unchanged in the decades before 1914. *n.d.*

4. COUNTRY LIFE – LATE VICTORIAN STYLE

This posed picture by Edward Reeves represents two important strands of idealised, suburban freedom: the 'rambler' and the 'sportsman'. Both are men from the town carefully dressed for the part – 'respectable' enough to enjoy the countryside without arousing landlords' suspicions. Specialist firms provided equipment for sportsmen: there were eleven gunsmiths scattered through late Victorian Sussex. *n.d.*

5. HARVEY'S OUTING
This picture is said to have been taken in Eastbourne. Workers in 'Sunday best', bound for an excursion. *n.d.*

6. DANCING IN THE STREET, HASTINGS
Not for any particular reason other than the visit of a wandering barrel organ. *c. 1910.*

7. BOGNOR

Sussex developed a number of small, minor resorts catering for quiet family holidays, each with its distinctive flavour. The first development at Bognor was Sir Richard Hotham's 'Hothampton' of the 1790s, a mile inland. The railway brought moderate success to seaside Bognor in the 1860s – quiet beaches, small-scale boarding houses, bathing machines, and overdressed ladies. *c. 1890.*

8. THE METROPOLE, BRIGHTON

The grand hotel was an alternative to the seaside home for the wealthy. The *Hotel Metropole* was built in 1888 of red brick and terracotta by the master-planner of 'gothic' public buildings, Alfred Waterhouse. The *Grand Hotel*, next along, 1862–4, was by Whichcord. *n.d.*

9. THE LEISURE CLASS

The Duchess of Cleveland at her Sussex house, Battle Abbey. She opened her home to middle class tourists, but complained of soda water bottles left in the shrubbery. *n.d.*

10. ELY GRANGE, FRANT

A picture from Pike's *Sussex*. John Waddington, J.P. seen at the wheel of the car, was a founder-member of the Automobile Club and High Sheriff for Sussex, 1909–10. He came from Leeds, trained as a civil engineer, became the 'original concessionaire of the Midland Land Grant Railway, and principal pioneer of the gold and coal-mining industries in that colony [Western Australia]'. The profits brought the house, car and membership of the Hunt. *c. 1910.*

THE PIANOLA-PIANO

Is the only Player-Piano which has the **METROSTYLE**, giving the correct interpretation, and the **THEMODIST**, which accents the melody.

Sole Local Agents:

LYON & HALL

WARWICK MANSION,
1, EAST STREET, Brighton.
Branch: 22, CHURCH ROAD, HOVE.

If you cannot call, write for **CATALOGUE H**.

11. SUBURBAN PARLOUR IDEALS

Photographs of small interiors were difficult to take. Then, as now, advertisements established the ideal. For those aspiring to the perfect tea party, admiration without strain, the piano played itself. *1911.*

12. 'DOMESTIC SCENES'

The enterprising Edward Reeves, in common with many other photographers, offered fantasy to his clients. A glance through the window gives the game away: the backdrop is artificial. *c. 1890.*

13. THE 'FORESTERS' ARMS', EAST HOATHLY

An extended cottage, rather than a purpose-built establishment. One of the many bought up by Harvey's, the Lewes brewers. Note the bicycles. The Cyclists' Touring Club was a major influence diverting the late Victorian village pub from its purely local interests, the forerunner of present-day drinking habits. *n.d.*

14. 'UNICORN COMMERCIAL HOTEL', BRIGHTON

The Unicorn used to stand at 133 North Street. As the 'Tudor' nameplate suggests, it was an older drinking house, typical of a small market town, partially adapted to the demands of the post-railway representatives of the Victorian retail revolution; the extension on the right provided for them. Edward Awcock and his staff ran it. Note the advertisement for the brewer, Smithers of North Street, and the bills of music halls and cheap excursions. *n.d.*

15. 'ROYAL STANDARD', BRIGHTON

A 'glamour pub' or 'gin-palace' to catch visitors to Brighton as they walked down Queen's Road from the station to the sea. *1899.*

16.   THEATRE, OLD STYLE

A bill for the *Theatre Royal*, in which the language is still essentially that of the eighteenth century. *1839.*

17.   SCHOOL THEATRICALS, HURSTPIERPOINT

An Edwardian performance of 'A Midsummer Night's Dream'. What influence the English public schools had on the growth of amateur theatricals and dramatic societies is an open question. Perhaps they were as important in this sphere as in games. *n.d.*

Brighton Musical Festival.

THE DOME, January 13th, 14th, 15th & 16th, 1909.

Jan. 13th, "THE DREAM OF GERONTIUS."
Conductor—Sir EDWARD ELGAR, Mus. D., Cantab.

Jan. 14th, GRAND WAGNER CONCERT.
Conductor—Mr. JOSEPH SAINTON.
New Suite. "Bon-Bon" (First Performance), conducted by the Composer, Mr. S. COLERIDGE-TAYLOR.

Jan. 15th, "ELIJAH." Conductor—Mr. ROBERT TAYLOR.

Jan. 16th, GRAND SYMPHONY CONCERT.
(At 3 p.m.) Including SIR EDWARD ELGAR'S NEW SYMPHONY.
Conductors—Sir CHARLES V. STANFORD (Mus. D., Oxon), Sir ALEX. C. MACKENZIE (Mus. D.),
and Mr. JOSEPH SAINTON.

At 8 p.m.) GRAND MISCELLANEOUS CONCERT.
Conductors—Mr. EDWARD GERMAN and Mr. JOSEPH SAINTON.

Orchestra and Chorus of 260 Performers.

Artistes—Madame AGNES NICHOLLS, Madame ELLA RUSSELL, Miss ALYS BATEMAN, Miss ALICE LAKIN,
Miss GERTRUDE LONSDALE, Mr. JOHN COATES, Mr. WEBSTER MILLAR, Mr. WATKIN MILLS,
Mr. WILLIAM HIGLEY, Mr. JULIEN HENRY, and Mr. W. A. PETERKIN.
Solo Pianoforte—Mr. ARTHUR NEWSTEAD   *Solo Violin*—Mr. PERCY FROSTICK.
Organist—Mr. PERCY TAYLOR, A.R.C.O.

Tickets at LYON & HALL's and R. POTTS & Co.'s.   For full particulars see bills.

In consequence of the Festival there will be no Orchestral Concerts in the Aquarium next
week, but the usual daily performances will be resumed on Sunday, the 17th instant.

18. BRIGHTON FESTIVAL

Music had been financed on a private commercial basis. The first Festival to
be aided by public money was this one. Elgar and Stanford; there can be no
doubt about its musical importance. *1909.*

19. VOLUNTEER BAND, LEWES PRIORY

Military prowess apart, the local Volunteer bands became a central feature of
late Victorian public celebrations. Their uniforms and music reinforced
English values. Only the Salvation Army could rival their attraction. *n.d.*

20. THE RIPE GIRLS' FRIENDLY SOCIETY

A group photograph of the village of Ripe's branch of the Girls' Friendly Society, set up in 1874 by the Church of England to provide recreation, help in finding employment and other facilities for young working women who had led 'pure useful lives'. This branch catered, in particular, for rural domestic servants and small-town shop girls. Firmly evident is the rector, probably the Reverend F. C. Fox. The setting was Edward Reeves' garden in Lewes. *n.d.*

21. 'VICTORIA GARDENS', BURGESS HILL
This pleasure garden was opened in the late 1890s. The boats and switchback were part of a permanent fairground. The party is All Saints' Hove Sunday School Outing, 8 June 1910.

22. BOYS' BRIGADE
In camp at Sompting, 1910, the Boys' Brigade combined the healthy enthusiasm of the Scouts with the uniforms of the Volunteers and the religious fervour of nonconformity. The emphasis on outdoor health was particularly important after the débâcle of the Boer War. *1910.*

23. THE EAST SUSSEX HUNT

Refounded in the 1850s for the East Sussex gentry, old and new, the Hunt operated in the Battle area, where it is seen at the start of a meet on the Market Green. *c. 1906.*

24. BICYCLES

An early picture of a craze Sussex shared with most of the Home Counties. Through the Cyclists' Touring Club, founded in 1878, these groups enjoyed the country's visual amenities and were a source of strong pressure for rural improvements and adequate signposting by the new District Councils of the 1890s. *n.d.*

Hurst College 1st XI.
1899-1900.

A. SADLER.   U. L. HOOKE.   S. H. JONES.   C. H. TAYLER.

F. G. FREEMANTLE.   W. SMITH.   D. N. MILESTONE   E. SHEARS   G. SMITH.
(Captain).

C. R. HEMSTED.   B. A. S. DYER.

25. A FIRST ELEVEN

The most common of Victorian sporting pictures. Groups were easier to photograph than action and such school photos were important for social bonds in later life. The Woodard Schools were very influential in spreading soccer in the county. *1900.*

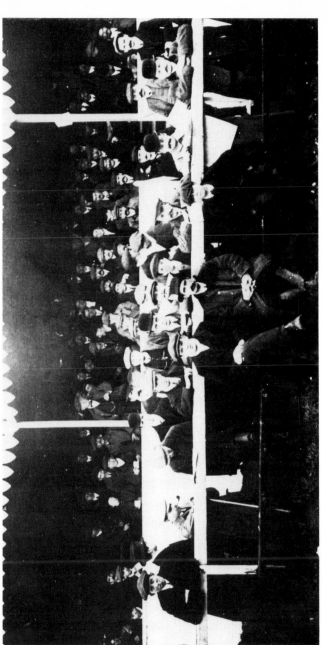

26. FOOTBALL CROWD, BRIGHTON

Photographing football was difficult. The action moved too quickly over too large an area for the average Edwardian photographer. So he photographed the crowd, advertising himself at the same time. The crowd does not seem likely to burst into mass hysteria, although it is known that they could. Note the women in the crowd. *1910.*

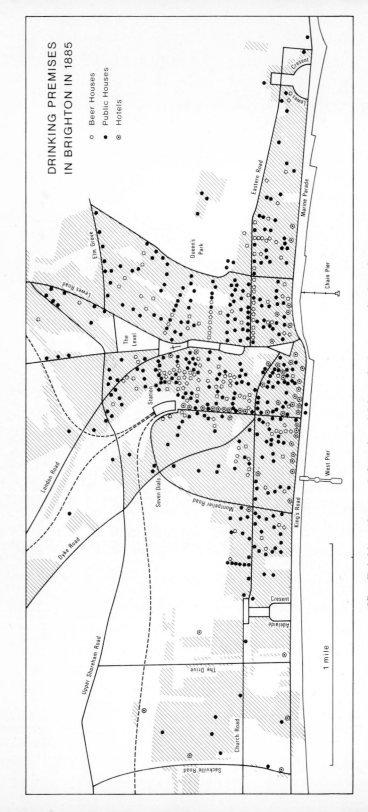

27. Drinking places reinforced social boundaries: note the beer-houses concentrated in older working class areas, and the less dense provision of larger public houses in the newer parts.

the five concerts included performances of *Cavalliera Rusticana, Samson and Delilah*, Act Two of *Flying Dutchman* and the Verdi *Requiem*. In addition, Sinding, Stanford, Edward German and Coleridge-Taylor conducted their own compositions, Marie Novello played the Liszt *E Flat Piano Concerto* and Sainton directed the 'first provincial performance' of Paderewski's *B Minor Symphony*. The *Times* judged the Festival 'a remarkable effort' and praised especially the newly-formed, 400-voiced Festival Chorus.[2] But the 1910 Festival lost £300 and proved to be the last of the short series. Sainton overreached himself by proposing for 1911 a performance of Strauss's newly-composed opera *Electra*, the mounting of which would have cost £1000, more than the entire cost of the first Festival, and would also have necessitated augmenting the 40-strong orchestra to 120 and importing continental musicians. The Town Council accepted the Aquarium Committee's recommendations against the Festival and in favour of a series of concerts on Wednesday evenings, which could involve the Festival Chorus, and Saturday afternoon concerts with visiting virtuosi.

Within a year the Municipal Orchestra reached another crisis in its brief existence. The weather was partly to blame, for the hot summer of 1910 had caused a sharp fall in attendances at the concerts, all of which were held indoors, a symphony orchestra being unsuited to playing in the open air. This fact brought demands from the persistent military band lobby for the return of the town band. At this point the Aquarium Committee lost its nerve over the orchestra, arguing that the cost had become too great — £4850 for the 1909–10 season and an estimated £5310 for 1910–11.

The proposal to withdraw support, however met weighty opposition in the local press.

> . . . it is all the more to be regretted that the Brighton municipality does not see its way to support another Festival or to keep going the excellent band Mr. Sainton has organised. Surely it should be possible, however, for Mr. Sainton and those who support him to found a South of England Festival, to be held alternatively at Brighton, Eastbourne and Bournemouth. It is the enthusiasm and not the talent for singing which is lacking in the South.[3]

Despite these optimistic suggestions from the *Brighton Gazette*, the orchestra was reduced in strength to 27 players for the 1911–12 season. It was also retained only from October to May, and as part of the same reorganisation, the military band was reinstated between the months of June and September. In this way the music bill for the year was cut from £5,310, the equivalent of a $1\frac{1}{2}$d. rate, to £2,980, an action which brought to an end a golden era in the history of music in Brighton. The plight of the orchestra affected their concerts. The *Brighton Gazette* observed in 1911:

> The mid-week concerts at the Dome now have a special and somewhat pathetic interest. At each, one hears works which can scarcely be given satisfactorily under the new conditions, and there are also contributions by individual performers who are severing their connection with the Municipal Orchestra. On Wednesday evening, for instance, there were Herr Abbas' cello soli Saints-Saens' "Le Cygne", Schubert's "L'Abeille" and Popper's "Papillons", – works which he played so frequently, and with such unfailing charm and artistic finish.[4]

Sainton resigned and was replaced by Lyell-Taylor,

previously conductor of the Buxton Spa Orchestra. The mutilated orchestra survived into the First World War and eventually even surrendered to pressure to give *al frèsco* promenade concerts, admission 6d.

The concert scene in Edwardian Sussex included other popular features. Private impresarios presented concerts by famous recitalists, which brought Dame Clara Butt and others to the county. There were dozens of minor piano recitals and such events as the 'Railway Guards' Concert for Superannuation Funds, with the string band of the Royal Marines (Portsmouth), the Westminster Singers, soloists and humour'. The military also made an important contribution to the musical life of the resorts with weekly or daily open-air concerts, the ideal background for promenading. The growth of this taste for music in uniforms is associated with the rise of jingoism in Britain during the 1880s, an enthusiasm which the Salvation Army turned to the use of Sunday religion. The 'influential classes' of Eastbourne subscribed to a visiting German band, but the minor resorts relied rather on the amateur bands of the Volunteers or the Fire Brigade. As a garrison town, Brighton was at an advantage when it came to putting together its summer programme of bands. In 1911 the 1st HCB Royal Artillery Band was the favourite. The Corporation maintained its own military band from 1891, as well as sponsoring promenade concerts by 'German Bands' in the *Pavilion*. However variable the military bands were in musical quality, they formed an essential part of public entertainment. The Victorian bandstand is their permanent memorial. Horsham's bandstand, erected in the Carfax in 1892, was an unusually attractive example. As a draw for the crowds, it replaced the gallows which had stood on the very same spot in the first half of the nineteenth century.

The professional bands and, briefly, the Brighton Municipal Orchestra both employed local musicians, who could also supplement their livings as church organists, schoolmasters, or as 'professors' in such institutions as the Hove School of Music, where the Brighton Municipal Orchestra's leader, Harold Ketelby, composer of 'In a Monastery Garden', taught. Further there was a growing demand for private musical tuition, especially on the popular pianoforte. *Kelly's Directory* for 1891 listed 130 teachers of music in the county, principally on the coast, but also in every market town, supported by 34 music, instrument and pianoforte dealers and 21 piano tuners. Most of their trade was for the home and it is this aspect of musical history which it is most difficult to trace. Drawing-room accomplishments were one of the greatest reinforcers of family-based Victorian respectability and the piano became a symbol, both of affluence and social accomplishment, especially in the parlours of the growing numbers of white-collar workers later in the century. The level of individual musical accomplishment was probably limited, and the repertoire restricted to the simpler fare heard at the Aquarium concerts, yet, in this spread of popular music for home consumption, the anxious young ladies of Sussex families and their suffering listeners contributed to the extension of an important new market for leisure goods and services.

The principal venues for public concerts in Brighton during the first half of the nineteenth century were the Music Room of the *Pavilion* and Mr. Child's *Grand Concert Hall* in West Street. These halls were augmented by various assembly rooms, particularly that of the *Old Ship Hotel,* and after 1878, by the *Aquarium Conservatory.* But the greatest addition came with the conversion of the Prince Regent's old riding school and stables into the *Dome* in 1867, carried out to designs by Lockwood, the Borough Surveyor. It provided a concert hall for performances on a scale never possible before, despite its acoustic deficiencies, exacerbated by the rebuilding in the 1930s, which have impaired performances there ever since. In Brighton the *Dome* was also supplemented at the turn of the century by the building of pavilions on the two piers, both of which were used for concerts. The other coastal towns could not offer the same choice of facilities, but they generally retained the assembly rooms of their past grandeur, acquired new public halls in the 1870s and also built pavilions on their several piers a decade or two later. Indeed, only Hove and Seaford were without a pier. Neither place lacked ready capital or willing enterprise for the purpose of building piers, but in both towns ambitious projects for piers in the Edwardian years were abandoned in the face of hostility from influential residents anxious to preserve for their communities an unequivocally respectable image of the seaside. As a substitute, Seaford used the *Albert Hall* for concerts, a private venture of Major Crook, and Hove used the *Great Hall* of Waterhouse's new Town Hall.

The building of these halls encouraged amateur and professional musicians alike, but the greatest boost to amateur music was given by the growth of music as a part of religion in chapels and churches. From an early date the chapels spawned numerous choirs which regularly assaulted their co-religionists with renderings of sacred favourites. In the Church of England, also, the growth of ritualism was particularly influential in the development of music, many people in Brighton being attracted to Sunday High Mass at St. Bartholomew's as much by the quality of its music as by Father Wagner's views on the place of the clergy. The rise of the 'popish opera' also had the side effect of creating professional employment for directors of music and organists who contributed to the musical life of the area by acting as minor impressarios and by teaching private pupils. The oldest amateur choral society in Sussex was the Brighton Harmonic Society, formed in 1827; it added 'Sacred' to the name after 1846.[5] Although the initial membership of the Harmonic was an amalgamation of the choirs from the Parish Church, the Countess of Huntingdon Church and the Salem Chapel, Bond Street, in terms of formal organisation it was itself independent of church and chapel. This self-help body was, however, supported in the early days by the Royal patronage of George IV and William IV. At this time an important musical coup was achieved with a performance of selections from Mendelssohn's newly-composed *St. Paul*, which took place in 1837, before its first complete performance in Britain. Thereafter, the changes were rung exclusively on the sacred repertoire, *Messiah*, *Creation*, *Samson*, *Judas Maccabeus* and *Elijah*. The Harmonic had its rivals, sufficient to provide during 1869 four separate *Messiahs* in the same year. In addition to this sacred activity there were other choirs with secular interests, such as the Hove Musical Union of 1868, which specialised in glees and madrigals.

The Sacred Harmonic took part in Kuhe's Festivals between 1870 and 1877, but the ambitions of the chorus master forced a rift with Kuhe who consequently founded his own chorus, the first Brighton Festival Chorus, which existed from 1877 to 1883. In the two seasons following the break with Kuhe the Harmonic tried to rival the Festival concerts, in 1877–8 with the *Seasons, Israel in Egypt* and *Messiah* and in 1878–9 with *Israel in Egypt*, Spohr *Last Judgement* and *Stabat Mater* and Costa *Eli*, all of which lost money. For a time the Harmonic fell back to modest presentations but discovered a successful formula for financing a year's activities out of an annual performance of *Messiah* on Good Friday in 1893, since when an unbroken run of performances have taken place. Handel was briefly overshadowed when the society tried Sullivan *Golden Legend* and Elgar *King Olaf* in 1907, but such programmes proved too adventurous for the regular supporters and financial considerations forced the Harmonic, after a final year of glory as the choir chosen for Sainton's Brighton Festival of 1909, to return to the old favourites.

For the Festival of 1910, Sainton organised his own chorus. 'The choir . . . possess a splendid quality of tone and have been admirably trained' wrote an enthusiastic *Times* critic.[6] The 'rich penetrating tone' and the 'attack and energy' of the performance of the Verdi *Requiem* more than compensated for the uncertainty about the notes in the closing fugue and a 'single false lead in the basses'. The performance was taken to the *Queen's Hall* London in 1911, and event of which even the *Brighton Gazette* approved, seeing it as evidence of the improving standard of amateur music in Sussex.

We in the South are apt to take it for granted that our singers are never equal to those in the North, but we must not let the

The reduction in the size of the Municipal Orchestra and Sainton's inevitable resignation led to the dissolution of this promising organisation. In its brief life the second Brighton Festival Chorus achieved musical standards and a prominence unrivalled in Sussex during the nineteenth century.

For longevity and quantity of achievement, however, the prize must go to the Sacred Harmonic which presented 228 concerts between 1846 and 1896, rather more than four a year. The informal impetus that religion gave to this musical activity came not only from the interest it awakened in the sacred repertoire, but also from the personal links between church attendance and membership of choirs. For example, the three chorus masters who successively guided the Harmonic between 1859 and 1915, for example, were each organists of local churches, Gutteridge at St. Peter's, White at St. Paul's and Taylor at St. Patrick's, Hove. In contrast, Sainton's successful Festival Chorus was a fully secular affair, trained by Sainton himself and willing to experiment beyond the traditional sacred repertoire. The Harmonic's progress, of course, matched closely that of religion and thus, it was hardly surprising that in 1921 the Society dropped the term 'Sacred' from its name, which marks a fitting end to the Victorian era of music in Sussex.

CHAPTER 7

ELEVATING INSTITUTIONS

The *Brighton Gazette* carried an editorial in 1895 which referred to:

> 'Fortunate Brighton'. Happy in the possession of a progressive Town Council, she is to be kept in line with the times; agencies of comfort and enlightenment are to environ the favoured and blessed, who, in due course, shall lack nothing that can be of benefit . . . she is to be partner in possession of a thousand elevating institutions.[1]

The editor went on to question the value of spending any public money at all on 'elevating institutions', in a way that marks an important change in attitude to the idea of improvement and, perhaps, even the end of an era. By the 1890s, indeed, the social strains of the industrial revolution were quite forgotten and the recent political conflicts of the 1880s had been stilled. Consequently the previous stress on the elevating use of leisure time, which to the editor of the *Brighton Gazette* seemed an extravagance, was to many people now simply an irrelevance.

Earlier in the century the new range of improving institutions had been for the respectable elements in society an urgent social and political necessity, both as a personal aid to advancement and as a general method of creating social peace and progress. But it had also proved possible to preserve social harmony by utilising the older recreational relationships and institutions, which still embodied the patriarchal responsibilities of pre-industrial England. The end-of-harvest suppers, for example, and, where they survived, employers' 'beanfeasts' for labourers and apprentices, served well the improving needs of the nineteenth century. By the same token, a novel recreation, the railway excursion, could also be put to use in a traditional social context. In the year of the Great Exhibition, for example, Mr. Smith of Rye took 60 of his labourers by train for an improving visit to the *Crystal Palace*. He marched them from the station to Hyde Park,

> Kindly pointing the various public buildings and other objects of interest presented en route . . . some of the passers by cracked a joke or two about their appearance.

Evidently, the slow rustics replied rather roundly, but generally the day went off well, in the words of the *Sussex Advertiser*,

> . . . not only an index to the kindness of heart possessed by the employer, but may also, we trust, be viewed as a testimony to the general character and worth of the employed.[2]

Philanthropic dinners for the poor, usually for children and the aged, were another customary event, commonly held in the winter months, particularly at Christmas time and the New Year, when charity could be more readily appreciated. But Lord Egremont held his annual fetes for the poor at Petworth in June.

> 3,000 women and children sat down to a profusion of the old English fare, roast beef and plum puddings. The men received no invitation, in consequence of some irregularities which had

been committed by them at the previous fete.

It is not known what the 'irregularities' had been in 1835 which upset this well-known benefactor of the West Sussex poor, whose emigration schemes had removed so many potential troublemakers to the colonies. Yet, all was not lost, for, in the presence of an estimated 20,000 spectators,

> At the conclusion of the feast, the remainder of the viands was distributed to the labourers, who were congregated in large numbers on the outside of the park fences.[3]

Schoolchildren and workhouse inhabitants, conveniently collected together in established institutions of improvement, were another favourite target of philanthropic effort. Two hundred and forty scholars of the Battle Langton Charity and National Schools, for example, 'were liberally regaled with a dinner of boiled beef, plum pudding and beer', followed by apples and appropriate lectures from the Dean of Battle on New Year's Day 1852. Similar events took place in the towns and were described in Brighton occurring at a much later date in the century.

> For some years past every First of January has brought with it a festivity well calculated to make a lifelong impression upon the crowds of juvenile participants . . . [for] there are many whose generosity of hearts extends to circles beyond their own comfortable sphere.[4]

'2,500 little hungry souls' who were fortunate enough to secure tickets were fed, once again, with the most venerable meal in the history of English eating, roast beef and

99

plum pudding. The infants on this occasion also bene-
fitted from

> ... the peculiar generosity of Mrs. Ross. For the last two
> years this patient and kind-hearted lady has been saving up
> all her threepenny pieces till they now amount to the sum of
> £5, sufficient to provide 400 children with woollen com-
> forters.[5]

Yet, the newspaper report also noted that hundreds of
children were turned away because this particular year,
1895, was a bad one for the Brighton middle classes,
who could therefore not be as generous as usual.

Whilst feasts and balls were commonly used in this
way as a means of reinforcing social bonds, they were
also organised by other groups publically to mark their
independent status. Annual 'blow-outs', imitating once
a year the daily habits of the aristocracy and the 'plu-
tocracy', were fostered by voluntary associations
whose founding purposes were often far from the pursuit of pleasure. There were, for example, many complaints that the Friendly Societies were merely covers
for regular boozing and feasting. But the Volunteer
Regiments afford the best local example of an organisation which developed many supplementary social
activities. The Volunteers were originally founded in
response to the invasion scares of 1859. They drilled
every week in fanciful uniforms as a preparation
against an enemy who only materialised when the
Boer War eventually exposed their volunteer amateur-
ism. The recruits came from the gentry and professional classes, the officers, as well as from
respectable tradesmen and artisans, the other ranks.

The non-military activities of the Volunteers were diverse, including bands of variable quality, church parades, football and cricket teams and annual balls and dinners. In 1894, the 1st Sussex Volunteers, Royal Engineers, 'C' Company, Seaford's weekly timetable was:

Monday 8.00 p.m., School, Recruits Drill with Arms
Tuesday 7.30 p.m., Town Hall, Band Practice
Wednesday 7.00 p.m., School, Engineering
Thursday 7.30 p.m., Town Hall, Band Practice
Friday 7.00 p.m., School, Recruits Drill with Arms.[6]

'C' Company's football team also had fixtures at this time against the Cement Works (Southerham), the Brighton Rifles and Lewes Town.

New clubs and societies for every purpose were formed in Victorian Sussex. In 1895 the Brighton Railway Foremen, the Prudential Assurance Company's local agents, the Royal York Habitation (no. 2457) of the Primrose League, the Licensed Victuallers and the Brighton Junior Association of Pharmacy each held celebratory dinners during February and March alone. The growth of these societies meant that good use was made of the many buildings newly erected for recreational purposes, such as the *Assembly Rooms* at Henfield and the many *Queen's, Prince's* and *Albert Halls* in towns throughout the County.

Earlier in the century, efforts were made to pursuade the poorer classes to set up improving, mutuality clubs of their own, although usually under suitable guidance. Churches and political groups, as well as individuals, were involved in this voluntary work, in which wealth, foresight and powers of persuasion were all valuable assets. Mechanics' Institutes, providing improving education to adults, caught on during the 1820s in the market towns, but they normally attracted members only from the trading and artisan classes. The 'Battel (sic) Mechanics' Institution', for example, was founded in October 1825, at an inauspicious moment when the town was suffering from severe agricultural depression and the bulk of its labourers were barely able to feed themselves, let alone join a club for the literary minded. The Institute struggled along for almost thirty years, with its library of 336 volumes, a rare facility in the agricultural Weald, acting at the main attraction. The winter programme for 1844 was typical of the activities of these organisations in Sussex.

> Several gentlemen have engaged to give gratuitous lectures during the ensuing winter, on Geology, the Poetry and Genius of Shakespeare, Chemistry, Electricity, Popular Delusion, and other subjects, to which the Committee respectfully invite the Ladies and Gentlemen of Battle.[7]

Thus, the Battle Institute exposed its members to the whims of the local antiquarian and the scholar *manqué*, as a pleasant means of alleviating the winter boredom of small market-town life, (rather than to systematic education in the Birkbeck mould).

Brighton and the other coastal resorts, for all their size, had few examples of organisations such as this. By contrast, in the big towns the tradition of public lectures was particularly strong, whether given by a local clergyman on some point in the classics or Edward Whymper or Fridtjof Nansen, whose appearances filled the *Dome* in Brighton. Moral improvement in Brighton, however, was most famously served by the greatest of the Sussex prophets of improvement, the Rev. Frederick W. Robertson. His relatively short stay in the town, until his death in 1853, was crammed with good works, firm exhortations to self improvement and successful efforts to create new facilities for this purpose. On the opening of the Brighton Working Men's Institute in 1848 Robertson wrote:

> We do not expect it will make the corrupt voter honest; it will not make the drunken voter sober, it will not make the selfish voter liberal; but at least it offers the means of saving the honest voter from the consequences of his own ignorance, and of rescuing him from being the passive victim of the demagogue, or being compelled to throw his vote blindly into the hands of his landlord or his employer.[8]

The charge for this process of improvement was only 1d. a week for each member of the Institute. Robertson's vision was wider than that of many of his contemporaries, refinement as much as utilitarian control was his aim, and, true to his time, Robertson introduced the language of competition into his defence of the Institute.

> Let there be a generous rivalry between your wives and daughters and this Institute. I tell them they have not got a rival. Let them try which has most attractions – a comfortable reading room, or a happy home.

Yet, Robertson was quick to quash political competition from the radical members when they proposed introducing anti-religious works into the library in 1850.

In order to draw more working men away from the

rival attractions of the pubs in particular, most of the Institutes and the Working Men's Clubs were forced in time to play down their stern diet of rational improvement, which they sweetened with more tempting items of entertainment. Dean Hook of Chichester was influential in this change, since he had seen the failure of the battle for the minds of tired operatives during his years as Vicar of Leeds. St. John's Working Men's Club, Brighton, therefore began advertising the 'Largest Bagatelle Board' in the town along with a library of 400 books 'to afford to members the means of social welfare, mutual helpfulness and moral improvement, industrial welfare and rational recreation'. St. Luke's Men's Club in the Mission House, Queen's Park Road, Brighton, was open from 7 to 11 p.m. every weekday evening, and, like all but the strictest temperance clubs, offered bottled beer for sale after the 1870s, although the members were limited to two half-pints in any single evening. In this way improving clubs were transformed into decent drinking parlours, and in this revised form, as safe alternatives to the pub, the county retained 35 Working Men's Clubs in 1896.

The reading rooms in the country districts of Sussex, however, were a category of institutions which stayed firm in their intentions to improve the populace. Most of them were established in the 1880s by local philanthropists and they represent an explicit, but unsuccessful, attempt to dissuade farm labourers from leaving the land in pursuit of work in the better-provided towns. Seventeen were in operation by 1896. The reading room at Bury, provided by Mrs. Currie, was combined with a club and covered skittle-alley and was also 'secured to the use of the inhabitants for ever by an Act of Parliament, 1874'. At Chailey there were newspapers and the indispensable bagatelle table, while Crowhurst's reading room was used for mothers' meetings. Fletching's was donated by Sir Spencer Morgan Morgan-Wilson, Bart. J. P., and Linch's was combined with a public coffee tavern and a library of 100 volumes.

Of all the recreational bodies pursuing rational enquiry, those flourished most which appealed strongly to middle-class members. Among the more successful were the quasi-political debating clubs and the societies which fed the Victorian passion for the science of classifying and recording. An example of the former was the Preston Literary and Debating Society, whose programme for 1906 included such debates as:

> October 8th, The Socialistic Tendencies of the Present Day.
> December 3rd, Municipal Trading.[9]

The most illustrious example in Sussex of the scientific society was the Sussex Archaeological Society, founded at Lewes in 1846. As an organisation, it appealed to people with sufficient leisure to attend afternoon meetings. One of Society's earliest regulations turned all M.P.s and Peers who became members into Vice Presidents, a practical move to attract patronage. One third of its members in the early days were clergymen, and a lengthy series of battles was fought between the serious antiquarians and those who merely regarded the Society as a pleasant genteel pastime. As M. A. Lower wrote in 1857;

> While the chronicle and the chartulary are by no means neglected, why should we obstinately repudiate picturesque

scenes, the joyous expressions of kindly feeling, the wine and the venison, and, above all, the benign influence of bright eyes and sunny faces, which are ever the concomitants of our charming anniversary?[10]

With 750 members and the Duke of Norfolk as President, this Society in 1907 was a success by any standard. Apart from archaeology, natural history was another subject pursued by scientific amateurs, and the Eastbourne Natural History Society was typical of this genre, with its enthusiastic and relatively affluent, although quite small in numbers, membership. There were further kinds of special-interest clubs, for example, the horticultural societies, which were formed in an attempt to inculcate more self-reliance among rural labourers after the debacle of the Swing Riots and the restrictions of the 1834 New Poor Law. Most towns and villages boasted one, and the rural poor were encouraged to plant good local strains of vegetables and other food plants. Many societies held annual exhibitions, normally in two sections, 'cottagers' with vegetable exhibits and 'amateurs' with flowers. Horticultural societies were thus an important antecedent to the late Victorian municipal allotment, followed in turn by the provision of individual gardens in artisan housing – not 'four acres and a cow' but a vegetable patch and an herbaceous border.

Religion had an ancient, if dwindling, claim on people's free time. The Religious Census of 1851, indeed, revealed facts about low attendances at services which shocked the religious authorities of the day. Many churches were spurred into increasing their congregations and organised secular attractions as a supplement to religious activities, including, later in the century, even athletic training and team games. Socially-minded clergy emphasised lay recreations both as a means to attract souls back to God and to re-establish their churches as community centres. Religious services themselves were also made more attractive. The protesters outside St. Paul's, West Street, Brighton in the 1860s, who complained about 'Popish Opera' (the ritualistic brand of high anglicanism fostered by the Wagner family and known as 'London, Brighton and South Coast Religion'), were on to a telling point. Apart from the pubs and cheap music halls of North Brighton, there was no better entertainment for the poor working man than the splendid rituals available to him free from the 1870s onwards, after the opening of St. Bartholomew's and St. Martin's.

The YMCA was an organisation spawned by, but independent of, the Church. Founded in 1844 there were eight branches by 1891 in the principal Sussex towns, which organised a wide variety of activities, from music and reading to games and excursions. As Dr. Kirby told the Brighton branch in 1895;

> ... (membership would) enable them, by a little economy and self-denial, to avail themselves of those aids to health and long life which formerly were luxuries with which only the rich were acquainted ... he strongly advised all young men to undertake some holidays either in Wales or elsewhere; and to get all the fresh air and exercise they could.[11]

The Band of Hope was another secular club closely related to the churches. The Rechabites held their national conference in Brighton during 1895, at which time fraternal deputations attended from The Sussex

District Council of The Sons of Temperance, The Good Templar Order, The Sussex Band of Hope Union, and the United Order of the Sons of Phoenix. Twelve years later, on 27 May 1907, the Brighton, Hove and District Band of Hope Union held a 'Great Demonstration, Fête and Gala' in Queen's Park, Sixty-three societies were represented, with a total membership of over 5,000. The programme included:

> 3.30 MIRTH and FUN
>   by members of the Volunteer Fire Brigade
>   Sports
> 6.30 SINGING CONTEST
>   Test Piece: 'Our Bands of Hope'
>
> Verse 1.
> Our Bands of Hope, we love them all
> How blest the mission, who shall tell?
> In virtue's path, the young are led
> To fight the cruel foe they dread.[12]

The list of improving organisations is endless. The PSAs, or Pleasant Sunday Afternoons, were a late-Victorian attempt to revive for workers and their wives the mission of the early adult Sunday Schools. Meetings took the form of an innocuous mixture of hymn singing, prayer and improving exhortations, but Robert Tressell made a characteristically snide judgement on the PSAs in *The Ragged Trousered Philanthropists*, his socialist novel about Edwardian Hastings. They attracted, he wrote:

> ... the 'religious' working man type. Ignorant, shallow-pated dolts, without as much intellectuality as an average cat. . . . They had to sit there like a lot of children while they were lectured and preached at and patronised. . . . Most

108

of them belonged to these PSAs merely for the sake of the loaves and fishes. Every now and then they were awarded prizes – *Self Help* by Samuel Smiles, and other books suitable for perusal by persons suffering from almost complete obliteration of the mental faculties. Besides other benefits there was usually a Christmas Club attached to the PSA or 'Mission' and the things were sold to the members slightly below cost as a reward for their servility.[13]

The bitterness of Tressell's condemnation is reserved for the respectable working men, who attended a church-inspired improving organisation. Working men also organised strictly secular improving entertainments, trade union fêtes, for example, but the labour movement was not without its own quasi-religious bodies. There were also the 'labour churches' which by aping religious forms of organisation successfully diverted religious feelings to political purposes.

Local government was another influence which shaped improving leisure from the middle of the nineteenth century onwards. The first official reaction to recreation in Sussex came in the seaside resorts. For a long time, Brighton had been conscious of its peculiar need to create an environment in which the leisure class could amuse itself without hindrance or risk to health. In 1839, the town began a 35 years' battle to move its sewage-disposal away from the beach, so that the promenaders would not be offended by the smell. Brighton also gave another kind of lead in the creative provision for recreation, when it purchased the *Pavilion* from the Queen in 1850. Thereafter, the building served not only as a tourist attraction, but also as a home for the round of dinners, exhibitions and balls which flourished later in the century.

Most of the other local authorities had a negative approach, however. Their contribution to improvement was to ban, or, at least, discourage 'disorderly' recreation. Battle, with one of the earliest Local Boards formed in 1851, occasionally broke out in a rash of restrictionism. It tried for years to stop itinerant fortune tellers, gypsies and other disreputable groups from using the Green opposite the Abbey gates, but the inhabitants of the town successfully petitioned to lift the bans in the 1880s. Again, the Board harassed the lively sons of local tradesmen who illegally extinguished the town's gaslights on Bonfire Night. The peak of its indignation was reached in November 1881, when it voted that:

> The attention of the Superintendent of Police be called to the frequent obstruction of the pavements by assemblages to young men and boys especially on Sunday evenings and the insulting language frequently used by them to passing females.[14]

The larger towns also did their share of harrassing, mostly with drunks and prostitutes as their targets.

Municipal intervention in the provision of libraries and museums is a more constructive story. Once again the spur was private philanthropy, and, perhaps, its outstanding memorial is the flamboyant *Brassey Institute* of 1878 in Hastings. Earlier, the *Fitzroy Library* in Lewes gave access to the public in 1862, for a reduced fee of 1s. 6d. a quarter, and, in Brighton, the former Royal Stables were opened as a library, museum and art gallery in 1873, using collections donated, once more, by private benefactors. In its first year of life, 40,957 books were issued, but for some years following the number fell, even though the service was free. Although an ambitious plan to build a Jubilee Lending Library in 1887 collapsed because of a lack of public support, the parsimonious Council did in 1889 open a separate reference section in the original building, whereafter book loans quickly rose to over 100,000 a year. The same building also housed an art collection and enterprising annual spring exhibitions, which aroused international interest, were held in the Edwardian period. The Museum, on the whole, acted as a passive repository for the curiosities of philanthropic collectors rather than as an agent of systematic collection or regular instruction. Yet such was the pressure of use on these arrangements, that parsimony eventually had to give way and modern buildings were provided in 1902, at a cost of £46,000.

Another bright spot distinguished Brighton from its neighbours, all busy building solid libraries and inadequate museums to house motley collections. This was the Booth Bird Museum – a collection put together by the scholar-gentleman, E. T. Booth of 'Bleak House', Dyke Road, Brighton. He originally bequeathed the collection to the Natural History Museum at South Kensington, but, since, since that museum had insufficient room to take it, the collection, together with 'Bleak House', itself was handed over to Brighton in 1900.

Most of the authorities could rise to a special challenge, but long-term provision for recreation was more problematic and Councils generally became involved only when the failings of voluntary effort were exposed. Lewes's open-air swimming bath, for example, was constructed privately in 1860, and passed into Council

111

control only later; its unheated waters remain a monument to self-mortification today. Healthy recreation was still a priority in 1890 when Brighton finally conceded the impracticality of winter sea-bathing and opened indoor swimming baths attached to the washing baths in North Road. Designed by the Borough Surveyor, they cost £8,000. At the opening ceremony, after a spirited selection from Mr. Pullen's Bijou Orchestra, the Mayor observed that this was the third attempt since 1861 to provide baths and was happily a successful one.

Local government also eventually took responsibility for providing recreation grounds and parks. Examples of private gardens, normally linked to private housing developments, such as the Kemp Town Enclosure at Brighton and the Devonshire Park in Eastbourne, were numerous after the 1820s. Parks open to the general public came into existence rather later in the century. One reason for this delay was that, in contrast to the smoky and unhealthy cities of the north of England, the age-specific mortality rates in Sussex fell early during the Victorian period to acceptable levels, which, together with the restorative sea and extensive open downland, belied the need for providing open spaces in towns. In practice, however, much of the countryside was not really available for casual recreational use because landlords feared poaching. Of course the country air was available from early in the century, but at a price, in commercial pleasure grounds. These developed in country districts close to the built up areas, Shoreham's Swiss Gardens, Hurst's Chinese Garden and Burgess Hill's Victoria Gardens, for example, but a visit was a treat not a necessity. The gardens, normally sited near country railway stations, were fairly popular, especially amongst Improving Societies in the coastal towns, who organised cheap excursions as a reward for regular attendance. The price of admission ensured that, unlike the seasonal pleasure fairs, enjoyment could be had without risk to respectability.

The question of free recreation space in Brighton was raised by the visit of the great Sanitary Congress in 1881. Angry ratepayers had blocked the Corporation's previous proposal to purchase Preston Park for £25,000 in 1876, but the Congress provoked new pressure which forced the Council into accepting the Park in 1883, at twice the original price. A gift of £70,000 from a W. E. Davies, deceased, covered the cost of purchase and some of the maintenance. Another public park in Brighton, Queen's Park – named after Adelaide, Consort of William IV – was laid out in the 1820s as part of an estate development designed by Sir Charles Barry, adjacent to the Royal German Spa, which had been opened in 1825. The Park was not intended as an 'urban lung' for public use, but as a private leafy setting for the villas planned on its periphery. Only two of the houses were completed, but the park served for many years as a fashionable promenade associated with the Spa, where chemical skill reproduced the mineral purgatives provided by nature in the Spas of Europe. Admission was by ticket – twelve shillings for the 1833 season. The Park changed hands in the 1860s, but it remained a useful private facility for the middle classes in the area. It was only when the Race-course Trustees eventually bought Queen's Park for the Corporation in 1890, that, as in the case of Preston Park, the intervention of an independent body stirred the Corporation

113

into action on behalf of the general public.

In 1897 Sussex, with the rest of the country, celebrated the Jubilee of the Queen's reign, although Battle was not able to express its support because of temporary lack of money. This Jubilee of Improvement was marked by fifty-three bonfires lit on the County's hilltops. In Brighton, the Mayor dedicated the Victoria Gardens, while the Volunteers fired a *feu de joie* and suitable sports took place. The *Brighton Herald* wrote about the sports that:

> It may relieve the minds of some rigid persons to know that kiss in the ring was only indulged in by a limited number, and it was of a decidedly mild order.[15]

16,000 Brighton children took part in the celebrations, but they were made to pay for their Corporation-provided tea with a display of mass exercises, led by a doubtless perspiring Town Councillor.

CHAPTER 8

FIELDS OF PLAY

The pre-industrial world enjoyed much of its physical recreation in boisterous pastimes involving animals. The common people of Chichester, for example, were described in the late eighteenth century as 'much given to mean diversions such as bull baiting, which was very frequent, and for which many bulldogs were kept in the town to the great torture and misery of these poor animals'. James Spershott further described how,

> On Shrove Tuesday the most unmanly and cruel exercise of cock scailing was in vogue everywhere. Scarcely a churchyard was to be found but a number of those poor innocent birds were thus barbarously treated. Tying them by the leg with a string four or five feet long fastened to the ground, and when he is made to stand fair, a great, ignorant, merciless fellow at a distance agreed and at two pence three throws, flings a scail at him till he is quite dead. And thus their legs are broken, and their bodies bruised in a shocking manner.[1]

Spershott's shocked description conveys his outrage at the cruelty involved in these primitive pastimes. It is also evidence of the general growth in sensitivity of feeling about such matters. This new tenderness had intellectual elements in common with the Puritan jeremiahs of the seventeenth century but now it was reinforced by the desire, on the part of an influential section of the population, to civilise men for the orderly tasks of industrial living. There followed a sustained effort to restrict

115

disorderly sports, the result of which was that both cock and bull-baiting, together with most of the other overtly cruel sports, were successfully harrassed into virtual extinction throughout the land including Sussex by the 1840s.

By no means all the pastimes involving animals, however, disappeared during the early nineteenth century. Horse-racing, for example, flourished in the prosperous context of the Victorian era, and, although its attendant gambling and low life drew considerable adverse comment, the status of racing itself was scarcely questioned. Victorian Sussex catered for racing with three courses, at Brighton, Goodwood and Lewes. The first races on the modern Brighton course had been held in August 1783 and thereafter they enjoyed aristocratic and royal patronage for over half a century. A crisis in the affairs of the race course came in 1849, at a time when Brighton's changing relationship with the world of aristocratic leisure was evident in other respects, the decline of the fashionable season, for example. Despite the withdrawal of aristocratic financial backing, horse racing was saved when Trustees were found to take over the course. The new management produced more effective organisation and built a new grandstand in 1851. Thereafter, the races took on a regular existence and the Trustees, absorbed by the corporation in 1894, ensured that in the 1890s Brighton had six days' racing a year, in a Spring and Summer meeting, with a large popular following, both from the local public and excursionists.

Hunting was another ancient animal-sport which survived throughout the nineteenth century, although not without vicissitudes. Whilst the West Sussex Hunt had a continuous history, the Hunt in East Sussex ceased to exist for a period, only being refounded in 1853, under the Mastership of Sir Augustus Webster of Battle, when it began to attract fresh support from newcomers to the countryside. The influence of people from the towns was a vital force for maintaining the older forms of country recreations in Sussex. Many weekenders took to hunting as a bucolic diversion from the strain of city-work, and membership of the Hunt became a mark of acceptance into county society. Even the famous Quorn of Leicestershire was saved by a millionaire shipbroker in the 1870s. As for Sussex at the end of the nineteenth century, Lord Leconfield's thriving pack from Petworth was still hunting five days a week during the season. Thus those animal-sports survived which not only escaped criticism for extreme cruelty, made no disorderly threats to property, but also enjoyed a measure of support from people from the towns.

Animals, however, played no part at all in the most notable Victorian achievement in the sphere of physical recreation, namely the development of a range of orderly and healthy games for men to play against men. Of course, human athletic endeavour was not invented in the nineteenth century. One highlight of the rural year in eighteenth-century England, indeed, had been the apprentice games. These commonly consisted of rounders in some places, and the various versions of football in others, but the adherence to strict rules was as unimportant as the pursuit of victory in systematic competition. In general, the games provided an occasion for communities to 'effervesce' and release tensions, normally under the influence of drink. It has also been suggested that they sometimes acted as a cover for protest against specific local complaints, representing a kind of ritualised form of collective bargaining. In any case, they were generally treated with a degree of forbearance by the authorities, perhaps because they were almost impossible to control with the primitive 'police' forces of rural England.

The Lewes bonfire celebrations were a good example of apprentice activity in Sussex. Games, as such were not involved, but the energy and social meaning of this idiosyncratic affair was not unlike that of apprentice games elsewhere. Until the 1840s, Lewes was usually the scene of a week-long riot, when the 'bonfire boys', a large, unorganised body of apprentices, labourers and general inhabitants, carried burning torches through the town, drinking and shouting. The windows of unpopular gentry and employers were usually broken. To liven it up, the 'boys' took to rolling flaming tar-barrels in 1829, and the mêlée grew in scale and danger during the troubled years of the 1830s and 1840s. The alarmed magistracy swore in hordes of special constables, usually terrified and extremely reluctant local shopkeepers, and took to calling for help on the Metropolitan constabulary, the only effective police force in the country. The battles that ensued reached such a pitch in 1848, the year of European revolutions, that the Earl of Chichester read the Riot Act from the Town Hall steps and dragoons from the local garrison-town, Brighton, were used to suppress the troubles. Threatened with a repetition of such tough action, the townspeople promised to organise themselves more peaceably and eventually formed the first of the new Bonfire Societies in 1853. Thereafter, under, rather than against the town's middle-class leadership, which included a series of fiercely anti-papal clergymen, the 5 November celebrations were confined to the one night and became the orderly, para-religious ritual which is still enacted today.

In general, however, the physical energies of men and boys were harnessed to the cause of social progress by athletic recreations more familiar to us than the membership of Bonfire Societies. The development of athletics overlaps with the history of self-improvement described in another chapter, but it had its own peculiar and powerful appeal. Games for individuals tested skill; in teams they encouraged co-operation and mutual reliance; generally, they satisfied a keen and growing taste for competition. Indeed, none of the Victorian virtues is missing from the list of benefits attributed to 'sport'.

The development of football illustrates these virtues in action. As late as 1888, an ancient variety of football was still being played just over the Sussex border, in Dorking, Surrey.

> On Shrove Tuesday Dorking, as usual, was the scene of a custom viz. football in the public streets, which has died a national death in the greater part of England.[2]

The modern version of the game, however, was introduced to Sussex in 1856 by a public school, Lancing College, which had developed its own rules, involving teams of twelve-a-side. Indeed, Lancing adopted standard soccer only in the 1870s, after the need for competition under identical rules had forced a clarification of the distinction between rugby and soccer. The respective national organisations which defended the two basic codes, were established for soccer in 1863 and rugby in 1871.

Most Victorian public schools combined an educational belief in the values of 'muscular Christianity' with a concern for the health of their pupils. Any crowded community, such as a boarding school, ran a serious risk of infection and epidemic and one way to avert this, particularly in the days of medical belief in infection by vapours, was to keep the boys occupied in the open air. And so football was taught as a means of healthy exercise, which pupils could also carry with them into later working lives in sedentary administration, the church and army service at home and abroad. Yet, it was the associated effects of football on personality and *esprit de corps* which were most fondly recalled by a master at Lancing.

> Lancing football was more than a mere string of successful matches. It was the greatest interest of the school at the time, and the hardness of the game, the emphasis put on team work, the demands of regular training, the inspiring influence of the coach, must have had great weight in the creation of those qualities which made this a golden age. It must have strengthened the belief of the school in itself and its future and helped to develop the growing consciousness of itself and its individuality. It contributed to that unity of aim and co-operation of effort which are the necessary conditions of positive result.[3]

Gilbert Jessop, the cricketer, was more specific about the circumstances in which a training in games would be useful in later life.

> . . . the greatest value of our school games is that they supply a field in which boys can be given responsibility. . . . If you have

pluck on the football field, it is not likely to desert you if you should be faced with business difficulties.[4]

Lancing's influence on the development of the game in Sussex was partly exercised through matches. Most of the College's rival teams in the 1870s came from other schools, such as Brighton College and Hurstpierpoint, and a few came from the new football and athletic clubs in the towns, the Brighton Athletic Club and the YMCA, for example. When the County Football Association was formed in 1882, it drew together clubs and schools with a predominantly educated middle-class membership for the purpose of co-operating over rules, forming representative sides, assisting with fixtures and, after 1885, running a cup competition. League competitions, with their harsh and relentless comparisons, were avoided in Sussex unitl 1896, when separate East and West Sussex Leagues were founded, with the Hasting, 1897, and Horsham, 1899, Leagues to follow. Yet, by this time, a social change had already affected soccer, which owed much to educational developments outside the public schools.

In counties other than Sussex, it is said that the poor learnt their soccer either from 'muscular priests' or from the sons of local industrialists, who had acquired their interest in the game at the public schools and the universities. It was a matter of educational chance whether rugby or soccer was taught, depending on the school or university at which the priests or sons of industrialists had been educated. In Sussex, however, the influence of 'muscular Christianity' was weak and there were few examples of paternal, industrial employers and of small industrial communities. Rather, the game

121

seems to have been popularised here through the influence of school teachers associated with the public educational system. Unlike the public schools, state schools were not allowed to teach games, only gymnastic drill, as a formal part of the curriculum before 1906. As early as 1882, however, the local schools were under pressure to introduce soccer. An 'open letter' to the Brighton and Preston School Board asked:

> Could such a scheme be set on foot by means of which the children . . . might be looked after a little on Saturday? . . . Of course it would be too much to expect the regular teachers to give up any part of their holiday but if volunteers were called for it is surely possible that some among the many who take an interest in the young would be glad to give a few hours on Saturday afternoon; for the purpose of arranging a game of football. . . . As things now are a section of the disbanded army of youngsters prowls about the streets, especially about the Market Place, eating rotten fruit, and doing themselves no good in any way.[5]

Several of the 'regular teachers', who had learnt to value team games in their own education, proved willing to teach soccer in their spare time, and so in 1892 the Brighton Schools Football Association was founded, among the first in England. Footballing enthusiasts in this way joined forces with those interested in keeping children out of mischief, to teach the game outside school-hours. Preston Park, recently purchased for the Corporation, was used for the purpose.

As a result, the number of players quickly increased and so did the teams. The Brighton teachers raised a team themselves, as did the Post-Office, the Cement and Iron Works at Lewes and the Southern Publishing

Company. Some of the new teams formed their own independent football clubs, but most were attached to existing organisations, the pubs, institutes and firms, which could help new teams with facilities and equipment. Other teams came from the Working Men's Clubs, and Hove's Working Men's Club even had its own ground. The largest industrial firm in the area, the Brighton Railway Company, produced several teams, the Juniors, Locomotive, Rovers, Stragglers, Wanderers and Wasps. The Volunteer Corps were also an important source of teams and the churches and chapels, seeking further to improve boys' habits and re-establish their own popularity, started to field sides against established clubs. Unfortunately, however, not every game was decorous. The Bognor Club for example, was even suspended for attacking a referee at a match with Worthing in 1894. The Saturday half-holiday was essential for popularising the game, and, by 1907, there were enough players with sufficiently flexible hours of work to form a Brighton and District Mid-Week League. The teams came from the police, transport workers, the retail trade, the *Hippodrome Music Hall* and other groups of workers who had free afternoons in the middle of the week.

As the social variety of people playing soccer broadened, so the sources of initiative in organising the game changed. The Burgess Hill Club, for example, had depended during the 1880s on players from the public schools and universities. By the end of the decade, however, the Club was finding it difficult to attract players from the traditional sources and it was also regularly losing matches to socially inferior opposition. In 1890, a merger was even proposed with a more successful team, the rival Burgess Hill Working Men's Club, but the offer was declined by the working men.

Another mark of the changing character of the game was the visit of a professional team from Nottingham in 1894. It beat the Sussex representative side 8 goals to 2 in 'the best exposition of Association Football given in Sussex for many years'. The difference between the amateur tradition and the recently-legalised professionalism could hardly have been more vividly demonstrated. Yet, professional football was delayed in reaching Sussex. Brighton as the largest town in the county was most suited to supporting a professional team and indeed, matches between amateurs had already attracted hundreds of spectators in the 1880s. Perhaps Sussex lacked the big industrial patronage and strong sense of vital community found necessary in the north of England for successful enterprise in football, because it was as many as thirteen years after the legalisation of professionalism in 1885, that the first team in the county to use paid players was formed in 1898. This was Brighton United, which played for one season at the County Cricket Ground in the Southern League. After several failures, the name of the team was changed to the Albion in 1902 and it eventually became fully professional, in 1904, when a complete set of players was bought from Dundee. Hastings also managed for two seasons to run a professional side in the Southern League between 1908 and 1910.

Of the other team games, it was cricket that developed most strongly in Sussex. It was a much older game than football even in its modern form and the nineteenth century saw many teams still based on village communities, for a game of cricket could contain on the field of play the social variety and the deferential relationships of the world outside the match. At the same time, however, socially exclusive clubs were also developing. The rule of the Henfield Club, for example, reconstituted in 1837, included the following clauses:

1. The society shall consist of members subscribing yearly, 5 shillings each, to be paid on admission.
2. The members shall meet on Wednesday at 5 o'clock precisely for the purpose of playing. If the Wednesday afternoon be wet, the meeting shall take place on the Monday afternoon following. . . .
3. Any member degrading himself and party by getting in liquor before the match is played out, he is under the forfeit of 2s. 6d.[6]

The size of the subscription and of the fines, together with the days, times and length of play, confirm the image of a club designed for leisured gentlemen. There was indeed a strong tradition of gentry teams playing each other at the county level, and the first Sussex representative side had been selected as early as 1734. One reason for the development of county competitions was that, unlike football, cricket always enjoyed a measure of national leadership from a dominant metropolitan club, such as the MCC.

During the nineteenth century, cricket benefited from the extension of competition which the rise of the railway made possible. Furthermore, in the summer the game began to play a similar educational role to football in the public schools. Despite its rural and aristocratic tone, the game also developed a strong following from spectators in the towns. Sussex, with its large population of retired and leisured inhabitants, was well suited to providing the patient spectators necessary for protracted matches, but the game attracted spectators from a far wider section of the population than this. In 1901, for example, a record crowd of 19,000 was assembled in Hove for a county match against Yorkshire. Spectator interest was also greatly stimulated by the visits of international sides, and their popularity was reflected in the great success of the Sheffield Park Cricket Weeks held in the 1880s and 1890s.

As an alternative to team games, there were the new sports that stressed physical fitness and individual effort. Golf, tennis and cycling were particularly popular with the late Victorian middle classes. Their recreations combined moderate exertion with social exclusiveness, maintained by the high price of sports equipment and the high subscriptions charged by private clubs. The membership subscriptions to golf clubs in Sussex, for example, was nowhere less than two guineas a year. Golf had been reintroduced into England in 1864 and spread quickly during the 1880s. Sussex had only three clubs in 1891, at Eastbourne, Forest Row and Littlehampton, but, by 1915, there were 36. Tennis and cycling had an even greater appeal, especially to the young and energetic. The wealthy played tennis in their own gardens or joined a select club, as in Hove.

On the east side of Somerhill Road, a little above 'Dunmore' is the Wick Lawn Tennis Courts, and at the top of Wilbury Drive, at the angle leading to Cromwell Road, The Select Lawn Tennis Club, organised in 1881, reveals its floral beauties. The eight courts are adequately sheltered by the foliage of the trees. The Club is essentially select, and members are selected only by ballot.[7]

The first cyclists came from social groups similar to

those of the tennis players. The early 'mounts' were expensive and difficult to ride, but the development of sporting competitions, together with a system of clubs, was successful in arousing interest in the new machine. Brighton, Eastbourne, Hastings and Chichester all had cycling clubs by the late 1870s, but the numbers of cyclists remained small. There were 20 members in the Brighton Bicycle Club in 1878 and 25 in 1879. A second club, the Brighton Rovers with 30 members in 1878, was rather more successful after changing its name to the Sussex Bicycling Association in 1879, when it increased its membership to 60.

Frederick Harrison, the local historian, was a prominent member of the Brighton Bicycle Club, even winning a 30 shilling racing prize in 1877. His bicycling diary, in which he noted all his journeys with the distances he covered, records a blend of sporting and touring activity. In 1878, Harrison attended several 'club meets' at the Cricket Ground, and, on one occasion, covered two miles in seven minutes, 'up and down the Madeira Walk'. In 1879, by his own calculations, he bicycled 409¾ miles in all, although the hilly terrain in the town caused him to travel the coastal route rather often. His busiest week was in July, when he went to Shoreham and beyond five times.

		Miles
Wed. 23	Findon and back and up and down parade	10
	Shoreham and back by coast	10
Thur. 24	Shoreham (back up road)	12
Fri. 25	—	
Sat. 26	Shoreham and back sea	
	Nearly to Littlehampton and back	15
Sun. 27	—	

Mon. 28 Shoreham and back Sea Road   10
Tues. 29 Round and about   12[8]

Harrison achieved all this on a penny farthing. As a result of the growing interest in cycling, however, the manufacturers began to improve the machines by making them simpler and safer to ride. The introduction of the standard 'safety' model, together with the pneumatic tyre, led to the widespread popularisation of the bicycle in the 1890s, during which decade more than one and a half million machines were sold. The bicycle even proved an acceptable form of transport for women, and its adoption introduced new freedoms for that sex. Vigorous advertising, the growth of a bicycling press, the development of specialist retailers and the rise of credit sale facilities further widened the social appeal of the bicycle. Cycling clubs remained important, but their interests switched from sporting competition to general touring. The Cyclist Touring Club, the leading national club, founded in 1878, still claimed 2 per cent of all cyclists as its members in the 1890s and it became an important source of pressure on the new County Councils for rural improvements and better road signs.

Today, indoor sports-halls have broken even the influence of the climate over open-air sport. In the nineteenth century, Saturday-afternoons and the clock replaced the agrarian season and the holy day as the time-keepers of organised physical recreations. Games that were shaped to fit the timetables and playing fields of Victorian public schools also found a place in the congested towns and busy working weeks of Victorian England. But the popularity of games also had crucial moral implications. Writing on football in 1899, M. Sheerman observed:

> There can too be no doubt that owing to the popularity of the game, public houses have been largely denuded and have surrendered their habitues to the more healthy enjoyment of the football fields.[9]

The best but inadequate evidence of who attended football matches in Sussex is contained in photographs of crowds, which suggest that the spectators were generally drawn from amongst the lower middle-class tradesmen and artisans rather than from the poorest working men. Nonetheless, both the large and orderly crowds at football and cricket matches, as well as the healthy players in Saturday- or Wednesday-afternoon matches, were proof enough of the triumph of Victorian values and virtues in the field of play.

NOTES TO THE TEXT

Chapter 1

[1] Smiles, S. *Self-Help*, London (1859, 1874 ed.), p. 19.
[2] Cited by R. Malcolmson, *Popular Recreations in English Society 1700–1850*, Cambridge (1973), p. 153.
[3] Perkin, H. *Origins of Modern English Society 1780–1880*, London (1969), p. 280.
[4] Marshall, A. *Principles of Economics*, (8th ed. 1920), p. 528.
[5] Cited by A. E. Dingle, 'Drink and Working-Class Living Standards in Britain 1870–1914', *Economic History Review*, 2nd ser. XXV (1972), p. 617.
[6] Gale, F. *Modern English Sports*, London (1885), p. xxiii.
[7] Beveridge, W. H. *Voluntary Action*, London (1948), p. 322; reference from Stephen Yeo.
[8] Myerscough, J. 'Recent History of the Use of Leisure Time', in Appleton, I. (ed.), *Leisure Research and Policy*, Edinburgh (1974), pp. 8–11.

Chapter 2

[1] Willis, N. P. *Pencillings by the Way*, London (c. 1835, 1942 ed. pp. 511–12).
[2] Mackenzie, A. S. *The American in England*, Paris (1836), pp. 273–282.
[3] Granville, A. B. *The Spas of England*, Vol. 2, London (1841), pp. 569–570.
[4] Bennett, Arnold *Clayhanger*, London (1910, 1947 ed.), pp. 476–477.
[5] *The Train*, IV (1857), p. 296.
[6] *Brighton Gazette* (henceforth *B. G.*) (8 September 1870).
[7] Hammerton, J. A. (ed.) *Mr Punch at the Seaside*, London (n.d.), pp. 158–159
[8] Anon., *Brighton, the Road, the Place, the People*, London (1862), p. 125.

9 *B.G.* (29 August 1895).
10 *The Graphic* (17 February 1870).
11 *Ibid.*
12 Anon., *Brighton*, p. 9.
13 Bennett, *Clayhanger*, p. 447.
14 *Where Shall We Go?*, Edinburgh (1879), pp. 20–21.
15 *Ibid.*, p. 56.
16 *The Queen Newspaper's Book of Travel*, London (1905), p. 11.
17 Day, G. *Seaford and Newhaven*, London (1904), p. 8.
18 *Seaford and Newhaven Gazette* (29 September 1894).
19 *Ibid.* (10 March 1894).
20 Perkin, H. J. 'The "Social Tone" of Victorian Seaside Resorts in the North-West', *Northern History*, XI (1975).
21 *The Graphic* (17 February 1870).
22 *B.G.* (30 September 1886).
23 *B.G.* (16 March 1904).
24 *B.G.* (2 April 1908).
25 *Ibid.*
26 *B.G.* (30 September 1908).
27 *B.G.* (21 November 1908).

Chapter 3
1 'Continental Travelling and Residence Abroad', *Quarterly Review*, 38 (July 1828), p. 154.
2 Duchess of Cleveland, *History of Battle Abbey*, London (1872), pp. 237–238.
3 *Ibid.*, p. 322.
4 *Ibid.*, p. 322.
5 *Ibid.*, p. 354.
6 Farncombe and Co., *East Grinstead and its Environs*, East Grinstead (1888); advertisement.
7 Tressell, R. *The Ragged Trousered Philanthropists*, London (1914, 1955 ed.), p. 81.

Chapter 4
1 Alberry, W. *A Parliamentary History of the Ancient Borough of Horsham 1295–1885* (1927), p. 353.
2 'H. of C. S.C. on the Prevailing Vice of Drunkenness', *Parlia-*

mentary Papers, VIII (1834, q. 3190).

3 'You Must Drink', *All the Year Round* (18 January 1864).

4 'Poor Law Report', *Parliamentary Papers,* XVIII (1834), pp. 489–536.

5 Burns, J. *Labour and Drink,* London (1904), p. 1.

6 'A Graduate of the University of London', *Brighton As It Is,* London (1860), p. 108.

7 United Kingdom Band of Hope Union, *Forty-Second Annual Conference Programme,* (1910); Brighton Reference Library.

8 'A Home Office Return to the Owners of Two or More Public Houses', *Parliamentary Papers,* LXVIII (1891), p. 193.

9 *The Licensed Victuallers' Gazette* (27 October 1899).

Chapter 5

1 *Sussex Advertiser* (2 September 1851).

2 Cited in M. T. Odell, *The Old Theatre, Worthing,* Worthing (1938), p. 148.

3 'A Playgoer' (Charles Fleet), *Reminiscences of the Brighton Theatre,* pamphlet reprinted from *Brighton Gazette* (1891), p. 14.

4 *The Brighton Season,* special edition of the *Brighton Standard,* (1904).

5 *Brighton Herald* (2 September 1911).

6 'A Graduate', *Brighton As It Is,* pp. 81 ff.

7 Brighton Alhambra, *Programme* (5 March 1900); Brighton Reference Library.

8 *Brighton Herald* (7 January 1911).

Chapter 6

1 *Brighton Gazette* (3 November 1853).

2 *The Times* (4, 5 and 7 February 1910).

3 *Brighton Herald* (28 January 1911).

4 *Brighton Gazette* (6 May 1911).

5 *A History of the Brighton and Hove Harmonic Society,* Brighton (1958).

6 *The Times* (1 March 1909).

7 *Brighton Herald* (28 January 1911).

Chapter 7

1 *Brighton Gazette* (10 January 1895).

2 *Sussex Advertiser* (14 October 1851).

3 *Sussex Advertiser* (20 June 1836).

4   *Brighton Gazette* (3 January 1895).
5   *Ibid.*
6   *Seaford and Newhaven Gazette* (1894); passim.
7   *Advertisement,* (1844); Battle Historical Society.
8   Robertson, Rev. F. W. *Opening of Working Men's Institute,* (1848); Brighton Reference Library.
9   Preston Literary and Debating Society, *Annual Programme,* (1906); Brighton Reference Library.
10 Lower, M. A., quoted by L. F. Salzman, 'A History of the Sussex Archaeological Society', *Sussex Archaeological Collections,* LXXXV (1946), p. 25.
11 *B.G.* (14 February 1895).
12 Brighton, Hove and District Band of Hope Union, *Fête Programme* (1907); Brighton Reference Library.
13 Tressell, *Ragged Trousered Philanthropists,* pp. 491–492.
14 Battle Local Government Board, *Minutes* (1881), (26 June 1897); East Sussex Record Office.
15 *Brighton Herald* (26 June 1897).

Chapter 8
1   Cited in Malcomson, *Popular Recreations,* p. 48.
2   *Sussex Daily News* (18 February 1888).
3   Handford, B. W. I. *Lancing 1848–1930,* London (1933), p. 298.
4   Jessop, G. L. *Outdoor Sports,* London (1912), pp. ix-x.
5   *Brighton Gazette* (2 November 1882); cited in D. G. Wilkinson, *Association Football in Brighton Before 1920,* (unpublished M. A. thesis, University of Sussex, 1971), pp. 51–52.
6   Squire, H. F. and A. P. *Henfield Cricket and its Sussex Cradle,* Hove (1949).
7   Porter, H. C. *The History of Hove,* London (1907).
8   Nairn, C. W. and Fox Jr., C. J. (eds.), *The Bicycle Annual for 1879,* (1879) Harrison's own copy, Brighton Reference Library.
9   Sheerman, M. (ed.), *Football,* London (1899), p. 173.

BIBLIOGRAPHY

Leisure history has seen a number of significant studies in the past decade or so and these have helped to furnish a framework of methods and analysis for our own approach. Apart from those works referred to in the notes to the text, we list the most important and useful studies below.

General

M. A. Bienefeld, *Working Hours in British Industry: An Economic History* (1972).

J. Burnett, *Useful Toil. Autobiographies of Working People from the 1820s to the 1920s* (1974).

L. Davidoff, *The Best Circles. Social Etiquette and the Season* (1973).

B. McCormick, 'Hours of Work in British Industry', *Industrial and Labour Relations Review*, XII (1959).

R. W. Malcomson, *Popular Recreations in English Society 1700–1850* (Cambridge, 1973).

H. Meller, *Leisure in the Changing City, 1870–1914* (1976).

J. Myerscough, 'The Recent History of the Use of Leisure Time', in I. Appleton (ed.), *Leisure Research and Policy* (Edinburgh, 1974).

E. H. Phelps Brown and M. Browne, *A Century of Pay* (1968).

J. A. R. Pimlott, *Recreations* (1968).

J. H. Plumb, *The Commercialisation of Leisure in Eighteenth-Century England* (Reading, 1973).

S. Pollard, *The Genesis of Modern Management* (1965).

G. Stedman Jones, *Outcast London* (Oxford, 1971).

K. Thomas, 'Work and Leisure in Pre-Industrial Society', *Past and Present*, 29 (1964).

E. P. Thompson, 'Time, Work-Discipline and Industrial Capitalism', *Past and Present*, 38 (1967).

'Work and Leisure in Industrial Society: Conference Report', *Past and Present*, 30 (1965).

S. Yeo, *Religion and Voluntary Organisations in Crisis* (1976).

Holidays

G. Hart, *A History of Cheltenham* (Leicester, 1965).

J. Myerscough, 'The Victorian Development of the Seaside Holiday Industry', in *Victorian Seaport*, conference report of the Victorian Society (1967).

J. Myerscough, 'Thomas Cook', in J. F. C. Harrison (ed.), *Eminently Victorian* (1974).

H. J. Perkin, 'The "Social Tone" of Victorian Seaside Resorts in the North-West', *Northern History*, XI (1975).

J. A. R. Pimlott, *The Englishman's Holiday* (1947; new edition with introduction by J. Myerscough, Hassocks, 1976).

B. S. Smith, *A History of Malvern* (Leicester, 1967).

J. K. Walton, 'Residential Amenity, Respectable Morality and the Rise of the Entertainment Industry; The Case of Blackpool', *Literature and History*, 1 (1975).

J. K. Walton, 'The Windermere Tourist Trade in the Age of the Railway, 1847–1912', in O. M. Westall (ed.), *Windermere in the Nineteenth Century* (Lancaster, 1976).

J. Whyman, 'The Growth of the Seaside Resorts on the Thanet and Kent Coast', in A. Everitt (ed.), *Perspectives in English Urban History* (1973).

Drink

J. Burnett, *Plenty and Want. A Social History of Diet in England from 1815 to the Present Day* (1966).

A. Crawford and R. Thorne, *Birmingham Pubs 1890–1939* (1975).

A. E. Dingle, 'Drink and Working-Class Living Standards in Britain, 1870–1914', *Economic History Review*, 2nd Series XXV (1972).

M. Girouard, *Victorian Pubs* (1975).

B. Harrison, *Drink and the Victorians: The Temperance Question in England 1815–1872* (1971).

B. Harrison and B. Trinder, *Drink and Sobriety in an Early Victorian County Town: Banbury 1830–1860*, English Historical Review Supplement 4 (1969).

136

Entertainment

A. Briggs, *Mass Entertainment. The Origins of a Modern Industry* (Adelaide, 1960).

C. Ehrlich, *The Piano: A History* (1976).

E. D. Mackerness, *A Social History of English Music* (1964).

G. J. Mellor, *The Northern Music Hall* (1968).

H. Raynor, *Music and Society Since 1815* (1976).

M. B. Smith, 'Victorian Entertainment in the Lancashire Cotton Towns', in S. P. Bell (ed.), *Victorian Lancashire* (Newton Abbot, 1974).

P. Young, *The Concert Tradition* (1965).

Improvement

G. Crossick (ed.), *The Lower Middle Class in Britain* (1977).

H. Cunningham, *The Volunteer Force: A Social and Political History, 1859–1908* (1975).

M. D. Fuller, *West Country Friendly Societies* (Reading, 1968).

A. D. Gilbert, *Religion and Society in Industrial England* (1976).

B. Harrison, 'Religion and Recreation in Nineteenth-Century England', *Past and Present*, 38 (1967).

J. F. C. Harrison, *Learning and Living 1790–1960: A History of the English Adult Education Movement* (1961).

K. S. Inglis, *Churches and the Working Classes in Victorian England* (1963).

H. Macleod, *Class and Religion in the Late Victorian City* (1974).

A. Summers, 'Militarism in Britain before the Great War', *History Workshop*, (1976).

J. Taylor, *From Self-Help to Glamour. The Working Men's Club 1860–1970*, Ruskin College History Workshop Pamphlet No. 7 (Oxford, 1972).

Sports and games

D. Brailsford, *Sport and Society: Elizabeth to Anne* (1969).

A. Briggs, 'The View from Badminton', in A. Briggs (ed.), *Essays in the History of Publishing: Longmans 1721–1924* (1974).

G. F. Chadwick, *The Park and the Town* (1966).

E. Dunning, 'The Development of Modern Football', in E.

Dunning (ed.), *The Sociology of Sport: A Selection of Readings* (1971).

D. C. Itzkowitz, *Peculiar Privilege: A Social History of English Fox-Hunting, 1753–1885* (Hassocks, 1977).

P. C. McIntosh, *Sport in Society* (1963).

J. Mott, 'Miners, Weavers and Pigeon Racing', in M. B. Smith, S. Parker and C. S. Smith (eds.), *Leisure and Society in Britain* (1973).

W. Vamplew, *The Turf. A Social and Economic History of Horse Racing* (1976).

J. Walvin, *The People's Game. A History of British Football* (1975).

Home

J. Burnett, *A History of the Cost of Living* (Harmondsworth, 1969).

M. Girouard, *The Victorian Country House* (Oxford, 1971).

P. Horn, *The Rise and Fall of the Victorian Servant* (Dublin, 1975).

A. King, 'The Bungalow', *Architectural Association Quarterly*, 5 (1973).

T. M. McBride, *The Domestic Revolution. The Modernisation of Household Service in England and France 1820–1920* (1976).

L. Davidoff, 'Mastered for Life: Servant, Wife and Mother in Victorian and Edwardian Britain', *Journal of Social History*, VII (1974).

S. D. Chapman (ed.), *Working-Class Housing* (Newton Abbot, 1971).

Countryside

S. Alexander, *St. Gile's Fair, 1830–1914: Popular Culture and the Industrial Revolution in 19th century Oxford*, Ruskin College History Workshop Pamphlet No. 2 (Oxford, 1970).

A. Howkins, *Whitsun in 19th Century Oxfordshire*, Ruskin College History Workshop Pamphlets No. 8 (Oxford, 1973).

P. Horn, *Labouring Life in the Victorian Countryside* (Dublin, 1976).

A. Rogers, *This Was Their World* (1972).

R. Samuel, *Village Life and Labour* (1975).

Sussex

J. Betjeman and J. S. Gray, *Victorian and Edwardian Brighton* (1972).

J. Betjeman and J. S. Gray, *Victorian and Edwardian Sussex* (1973).

B. Copper, *A Song for Every Season* (1971).

A. Dale, *Fashionable Brighton 1820–1860* (1947 and, Newcastle, 1969).

E. W. Gilbert, *Brighton Old Ocean's Bauble* (1954 and, Hassocks, 1975).

J. Lowerson, *Victorian Sussex* (1972).

J. Lowerson, *An Embryonic Brighton: Victorian and Edwardian Seaford* (Brighton, 1975).

Sociology

I. Appleton (ed.), *Leisure Research and Policy* (Edinburgh, 1974).

A. Clayre, *Work and Play. Ideas and Experience of Work and Leisure* (1974).

J. Dumazedier, *Towards a Society of Leisure* (New York, 1967).

S. B. Linder, *The Harried Leisure Class* (New York, 1970).

S. R. Parker, *The Future of Work and Leisure* (1972).

K. Roberts, *Leisure* (1970).

M. B. Smith, S. R. Parker and C. S. Smith (eds.), *Leisure and Society in Britain* (1973).

M. Young and P. Willmott, *The Symetrical Family: A Study of Work and Leisure in the London Region* (1973).

A NOTE ON THE PHOTOGRAPHS

Professional photographers first worked in Sussex in the 1860s, and they undoubtedly took the best surviving photographs of life in the Victorian and Edwardian county. The early techniques of photography, however, put serious limits on both subject matter and location, and so only a few photographs in this book date from the earliest days. The first photographers were heavily encumbered by equipment, and the need to paint each glass plate with bromide before exposure seriously restricted their mobility. The necessity for human subjects to freeze for up to half a minute also effectively precluded 'action' shots of leisure activities. Indeed, it was not until the mass production of the dry gelatine plate in the 1870s that photographers were really liberated from their studios.

Outstanding among the Sussex collections of photographs are those taken by Edward Reeves of Lewes, which are now kept in the Library of the Sussex Archaeological Society. His career was typical. Born in Benenden, Kent, in 1824, he settled in Lewes as a watchmaker and jeweller in 1858 at 68 High Street. After a partnership with James Russell, the brother of the court photographer, Reeves added 'photographic artist' to his advertised skills and by 1867 was in business solely as a photographer at 159 High Street, the present address of the surviving family firm. Until his death in

1905, he regularly photographed the people and environs of Lewes as well as his studio clients. It is unfortunate that many of his surviving plates are undated and unnamed. Walter Fry of Brighton, whose photographs form an important part of the Hove Library's collection, was another successful professional photographer whose work was varied in style and subject. In contrast to the professional photographers, little of the work of Victorian amateur photographers survives in public archives. Useful collections are owned by private institutions such as Hurstpierpoint College, where they give a fascinating record of work and play over a long period. But it is a pity that more of the many Victorian photographs taken by amateurs that surely must exist in private hands have not found their way into public archives.

Sussex took part in Sir Benjamin Stone's National Photographic Record, begun in 1897. The county's contribution was dominated by the interests of the Sussex Archaeological Society up to the collapse of the project in 1906, which is one reason why the local collection, now deposited in the Brighton Reference Library, was concerned almost entirely with church architecture. People are pictured only rarely on these plates. Indeed, this limitation of subject matter is an important general defect of photographs as an historical source. The Victorian photographers of Sussex concerned themselves more with places than with people, and only in formal groups and individual portraits did they catch people at their boring best. Frith, perfectly correctly, excluded people almost totally from his famous topographical postcards, and technical limitations kept people out of informal interior shots. Social behaviour, in other words, was rarely pictured. Sussex, in contrast with other areas, also lacked a photographer who exploited the reforming and news value of low-life scenes. These are further reasons why local 'action' photographs of many interesting scenes such as drinking in pubs, theatrical performances, musical entertainments, fairs and indoor domestic life, are largely absent from these pages.

Even 'posed' photographs, however, do convey to past places and faces a realism that is not always spurious, and, as icons, they can be inspected for evidence of values, aspirations and self-awareness of those who collected them and of the groups and the individuals whom they depict. Photographs, like other historical sources, need interpretation to make them more than merely entertaining antiquarian cyphers, and we do hope that this book provides a little of that interpretation.

INDEX

145

147